INVESTING WITH

Intelligent ETFs

INVESTING WITH
Intelligent ETFs

*Strategies for
Profiting from
the New Breed
of Securities*

BY MAX ISAACMAN

New York   Chicago   San Francisco   Lisbon   London   Madrid
Mexico City   Milan   New Delhi   San Juan   Seoul
Singapore   Sydney   Toronto

The *McGraw·Hill* Companies

1 2 3 4 5 6 7 8 9 0   DOC/DOC   0 1 0 9 8

ISBN: 978–0–07–154389–7
MHID: 0–07–154389–9

This publication is designed to provide accurate and authoritative information in regard to the subject matter covered. It is sold with the understanding that neither the author nor the publisher is engaged in rendering legal, accounting, or other professional service. If legal advice or other expert assistance is required, the services of a competent professional person should be sought.

—*From a Declaration of Principles jointly adopted by a Committee of the American Bar Association and a Committee of Publishers*

McGraw-Hill books are available at special quantity discounts to use as premiums and sales promotions, or for use in corporate training programs. For more information, please write to the Director of Special Sales, Professional Publishing, McGraw-Hill, Two Penn Plaza, New York, NY 10121–2298. Or contact your local bookstore.

Library of Congress Cataloging-in-Publication Data

Isaacman, Max.
    Investing with intelligent ETFs / by Max Isaacman.
       p. cm.
    Includes indexes.
    ISBN-13: 978-0-07-154389-7
    ISBN-10: 0-07-154389-9
    1. Exchange traded funds. 2. Investments. I. Title.
HG6043.I83 2008
332.63'27–dc22
                                            2008031046

DEDICATION

This book is dedicated to the late Sylvia Clough of San Francisco, a past president of the Nob Hill Association and the Comstock Apartment Board of Directors, who was a caring, selfless, and tireless worker for people in her community. Sylvia inspired everyone who met her to reach for the stars, including at least one little boy.

CONTENTS

DISCLAIMER

I own ETFs for myself and also for my clients, and I have written about many of these in this book. There are risks in investing in ETFs and in the stock and bond markets. There are no guarantees you will make money in the stock markets, and everyone knows you could lose money.

Most ETFs covered in this book are those that are constructed using equity securities. Other ETFs described employ derivatives and other instruments to attempt to replicate, before fees and expenses, the performance of an index or price changes of a currency.

This book gives no legal or tax advice. Every investor and trader has his or her own risk profile and objectives. Read the prospectus of the ETFs you are interested in, which can usually be downloaded from the ETF maker's Web site.

FOREWORD

Exchange-Traded Funds (ETFs) are one of the most innovative and exciting financial products ever introduced. ETFs borrow some of the best features of stock and mutual fund investing to offer a broadly distributed portfolio management and trading tool that has transformed the way we invest.

When Max asked me to write the Foreword for this book in which he examines many of the new ETF products to bring them into focus for individual investors, I was thrilled to have the opportunity to support his efforts to make some of these ETFs more accessible.

I have spent the past decade working at the American Stock Exchange in the ETF division, assisting large traditional issuers and entrepreneurial start-ups in bringing new and innovative products to the marketplace and educating the investment community about the ETF category.

With the aggressive growth in the ETF industry, it has been an extremely exciting time, and I am fortunate to have been directly involved in the hundreds of ETFs that have listed on the American Stock Exchange (AMEX) since my arrival.

My passion and enthusiasm for ETFs began during the relatively early stages of the ETF market, and like many others from the AMEX and the ETF industry, it brings me great joy to see how successful and widely recognized the current ETF products have become. Even though ETF has become more of a household word than many ever imagined, basic information on ETFs is still unknown to many investors. Some existing ETF investors need to learn about the variations in products and the new, more specialized, and complex ETFs. This book will bring increased awareness to these new products and educate investors on the diversity of this industry.

As the investor base for ETFs has become more diverse, customer appetite for a greater array of investment solutions has sparked ETF issuers to expand the universe of portfolios that are delivered through ETFs.

Remarkably, the large, dynamic market for ETFs in the United States evolved from a single product, the Standard and Poor's Depositary Receipts (SPDRs), which are based on the S&P 500 Index, and which were launched on the American Stock Exchange in 1993.

The ETF market's early expansion resulted primarily from the success of the small number of available products. The expansion continued through the slow and steady addition of new ETF products. These securities are based on other traditional benchmark indexes for domestic and international stock markets, indexes for specific market sectors and capitalization ranges of the stock market, and broad exposure to domestic bond markets. Many of these early institutional benchmark products formed a foundation for the success of ETFs, and these products and their issuers will continue to be the core drivers for the future asset growth of the ETF market.

The recent explosion of new ETF products has been characterized by differentiated and highly specialized offerings, in terms of asset class, index methodology, and designated index exposure. A large number of new issuers, start-ups as well as established investment managers and distributors, have entered the ETF market in the past few years, so you can expect to see a wide variety of new investment solutions offered as ETFs.

Within the past five years, many new indexes for ETFs have been created that use novel component selection and/or weighting methods to construct index portfolios.

These enhanced or strategic indexes may sometimes seem at odds with the traditional concepts of low turnover and broad market coverage that are embodied in most benchmark indexes widely adopted by asset managers. But as ETFs are used more and more by retail investors and their advisors, they have become a natural extension of the index market.

Many ETF and index providers recognize the value of being able to deliver indexes with unique component selection and weighting processes that are likely to resonate with distinct groups of investors and advisors, especially those who have come to appreciate the transparency and tradability of ETFs. These investors still seek products with some of the attributes or processes more typically used in the stock selection and weighting of managed portfolios and mutual funds, and they are also hoping to find potential performance gains relative to a traditional index benchmark.

The trading flexibility and diversification offered with ETFs make them particularly effective for providing sector and industry exposures. Many popular products have been introduced that target narrow industry segments of the market or hit on a specific theme that may cut across traditional industry groupings, such as alternative energy and water.

Some ETF providers have also launched new ETFs that track the performance of a variety of specialty indexes that incorporate screens designed to meet other common investor criteria, including socially responsible investment mandates and dividend yield screens.

Quantitative screening processes, alternative weighting methods such as equal weighting or weightings based on fundamental factors, and rigorous screening processes to assemble portfolios that include companies incorporating unique information sets or expertise have been used by individual investors and professional asset managers alike. These processes are also frequently used in other financial products such as unit investment trusts, mutual funds, managed accounts, and structured products.

These approaches have all proved to be well-suited for the discipline and transparency of index construction and the distribution power of ETFs.

Just as the ETF structure incorporated features from other investment vehicles, the investment objectives and processes that prove to be successful in those financial products will be a source for new ETF ideas. The advantages of ETFs have also inspired innovations in indexing that are being implemented as ETFs first and then later offered in other investment products.

In order to offer ETFs for some of these asset classes, variations in product structures have been used to provide investors with many ETF-like attributes while using grantor trusts, commodity pools, partnerships, and other legal structures instead of the traditional fund structure.

In addition to having ETFs track benchmarks for different asset classes and strategic or specialized indexes, the market has recently seen the introduction of a large number of successful ETF products that offer investors exposure to the inverse, multiple, or inverse multiple performance of an index on a daily basis. The wider array of asset categories and new varieties of products with unique index construction processes or internally leveraged index exposures open new possibilities for investment strategies that individuals and institutions can employ using ETFs.

As ETFs have expanded to meet investor demands for new asset classes and exposures, new product offerings have been supported by an increase in understanding and acceptance by investment advisors and individual investors.

ETF industry participants will need to continue to promote investor awareness and understanding of ETFs in order to provide a platform for distributing a growing number and variety of new ETFs that include increasingly specialized and complex products as well as the traditional products that built and defined the category.

Since 1993, the ETF market has experienced extraordinary growth in assets under management, trading volume, investor awareness, and number of products. It appears that the industry is poised for continued success through increasing investor usage of existing products and broadening investment choices.

The luxury of having more investment choices carries with it a need for additional education and research. This book will introduce some of the many new ETFs and ETF providers and help investors quickly understand many of the unique products that are changing the ETF landscape. These products will be the engines for the next phase of growth in investor usage of ETFs.

Scott Ebner
Senior Vice President, ETF Marketplace
American Stock Exchange
September 2007, New York

ACKNOWLEDGMENTS

Thanks to Jeanne Glasser and Morgan Ertel at McGraw-Hill for help in fashioning this book into its best form. Also Dianne Wheeler and Judy Schuler for their editing help. Thanks to my wife, Joyce Glick, and family.

My associates at East/West Securities in San Francisco were helpful and shared my enthusiasm in getting this information out to investors and traders: Dr. Charles Chen, Leslie U. Harris, Bennie Choi, and Wilson Chow.

Many financial professionals gave of their time and energy to help: Laura Libretti, McGraw-Hill; Christine Hudacko and Peggy Mew, BGI; Mary Chung and Scott Ebner, AMEX; Rob Arnott, Research Affiliates, LLC; Cleve Rueckert, Birinyi Research; John Southard, Bruce Bond, Andy Schmidt, PowerShares Capital Management; Louis-Vincent Gave, Steven C. Vannelli, Pierre Gave, GaveKal Capital, LLC; Terri Berg, William Seale, ProFund Advisors, LLC; Matt Bennett, Third Way: A Strategy Center for Progressives; Julie Silcox, Luciano Siracusano, Professor Jeremy J. Siegel, WisdomTree Investments, Inc.; Tim Halter, Halter Financial Group; Michael Byrum, Tim Meyer, Rydex Investments.

INVESTING WITH
Intelligent ETFs

INTRODUCTION

The book you are holding is an invaluable resource for every investor and trader, from people who know nothing about investments to people who have invested and traded for years. By reading this book you will not only see how indexing can often help you beat most professional stock pickers but you will also learn about new ETFs. These include the ETFs that seek to replicate the performance, not counting fees and expenses, of intelligent indexes. Also covered are magnified-return ETFs, which offer the potential of twice the return of an index, but, of course, there is also twice the risk. There are ETFs that allow you to short indexes, with the potential of one or two times, giving you the tools to create your own hedge fund. You will learn how to use ETFs that track fundamentally weighted indexes as opposed to the traditional first-generation indexes, which are usually a variation of cap-weighted.

The new securities are constructed to outperform the original indexes. The original indexes are effective, but this book will show alternative investments that can add alpha to a portfolio. I've included figures throughout that document the compelling track records of the new securities.

THE NEW ETFs

There are now ETFs that track indexes of currencies and commodities and other specialized, alternative ETFs that have a low correlation to the stock market. There are also ETFs for BRIC countries (Brazil,

Russia, India, China), which are the fastest growing regions in the world. These new ETFs enable you to execute strategies previously available only to the most sophisticated investors. For example, you can buy the Russell 2000 Index on a magnified basis, which would possibly increase the return from this index by about 200 percent, or you can short the Russell 2000 on a magnified basis. You can now buy ETFs that provide exposure to developed and emerging foreign markets. If you think that these markets are overpriced or that markets worldwide are going lower, there are ETFs that allow you to short these countries and regions.

The new securities have revolutionized today's marketplace by making these investment and trading strategies available to everyone, not just the most sophisticated investor. This book will show you how ETFs are constructed and how this form of investing is superior to buying stocks or mutual funds.

SEARCHING FOR ALPHA

Investors and traders are now seeking alpha in their market activity to outperform the long-term average yearly return of the S&P 500. *Alpha* is a calculation of the risk-adjusted performance of a security. The reason to search for alpha is that investors got used to getting high double-digit returns in the late 1990s, when tech exuberance took the market to new highs. We are now in sideways markets where simply buying and holding may not give that sort of return. Also, interest rates were higher in the early 1980s, and investors could buy bonds to augment their stock market return.

This performance is hard to achieve. From 1926 through March 2007, the S&P 500 Index has had a compounded average return of

10.46 percent per year, counting dividends and reinvesting these dividends, and not counting taxes or other expenses (source: Standard and Poor's). In the total return, 40.6 percent was in the form of dividends.

Before you invest, keep in mind how much you want to make versus the risk you can afford to take, both financially and emotionally, and have some sense of your financial abilities.

If you want a higher return than the market usually gives, you should keep alpha in mind as you search. A high alpha value means that the security will perform better than expected in relation to its beta, or volatility. Because of its higher potential there is generally more risk in higher-alpha stocks or indexes.

Rydex Investments has done studies that show that markets move in cycles. Over the last 110 years the market has experienced four bull markets and four bear markets. Over that time there have been 42 years of bull markets and 60 years of bear markets. The per-year annualized returns in the bull cycles have ranged from 8.72 to 30.44 percent, while the bear years showed returns of −.24 to a return of 0.98 percent.

This return favors the bulls since returns were higher in the bull years than the lows of the bear years. But since markets move in cycles, investors and traders may want to reach for alpha to get better returns in the down to sideways cycles. Unfortunately, you won't know which cycle you're in until you look back after the cycle has shifted.

Also, alpha seekers can use short ETFs to get better returns in down to sideways markets, either of the magnified or nonmagnified type.

Or, if an investor or trader merely wants to attempt to outperform the S&P 500 or another index, she can use an intelligent ETF such as one that replicates a fundamentally weighted index. These are constructed to reflect the value of companies in an index other than merely using cap-weighted methodology.

THE INDEX REVOLUTION

Since I wrote the groundbreaking book about Exchange Traded Funds (ETFs), *How to be an Index Investor* (McGraw-Hill, 2000), almost eight years ago, investing and trading in ETFs has exploded. The number of ETFs has grown, too: in 2000 there were approximately 15 ETFs, and as of this writing there are hundreds worldwide.

The reason to index through ETFs rather than try to beat the market by buying individual stocks is as true now as it was when I wrote *How to be an Index Investor*: usually indexes in many cap sizes and styles beat stocks picked by professionals. Barclays Global Investors (BGI) has published information showing that from December 31, 1996, to December 31, 2006, 96 percent of large-cap value managers underperformed their index on an after-tax basis. Eighty-six percent of the large-cap blend managers underperformed their indexes, and 56 percent underperformed in the large-cap growth category. In all the mid-cap categories and the small-cap value category, stock pickers also underperformed.

Because of the interest in indexing the first wave of ETFs, the Nasdaq 100 (symbol QQQQ), the S&P 500 (symbols SPY or IVV), Dow Jones Industrial Average (symbol DIA), and others were created. The current wave of ETFs are based on intelligent indexes, which are constructed to be more risk averse and perform better than the original ETFs. This group includes fundamentally weighted indexes, which are contrasted with cap-weighted indexes; index-based ETFs that are leveraged, either on the short or the long side of the market; and other ETFs, which are constructed to be noncorrelated or have little correlatation to the stock market.

INTELLIGENT INDEX PERFORMANCE

Look at Figure I.1, which compares the Dynamic Market Intellidex Index to the S&P 500 Index, backdating it as if it had been an ETF. PowerShares offers an ETF that seeks to replicate the performance of

Figure I.1[1]

PWC, Dynamic Market Intellidex vs. SPY S&P 500 1995–2006

Source: PowerShares Capital Management

[1] Total Returns are based on the Closing Market Price. Performance data quoted represents past performance, which is not a guarantee of future results. Investment returns and principal value will fluctuate, and shares, when redeemed, may be worth more or less than their original cost. Current performance may be higher or lower than performance data quoted. After-tax returns reflect the highest federal income tax rate but exclude state and local taxes. Fund performance reflects fee waivers, absent which, performance data quoted would have been lower.

The Dynamic Market Intellidex Index return does not represent the fund return. The performance results shown are hypothetical and reflect the investment returns that might have been achieved by investing $10,000 according to the index on July 31, 1995. The results assume that no cash was added to or assets withdrawn from the hypothetical investment and that all dividends, gains, and other earnings in the account were reinvested in accordance with the index's rules. The Dynamic Market Intellidex Index does not charge management fees or brokerage expenses, and no such fees or expenses were deducted from the hypothetical performance shown. The index does not lend securities, and no revenues from securities lending were added to the performance shown. You cannot invest directly in the index. In addition, the results actual investors might have achieved would have differed from those shown because of differences in the timing, amounts of their investments, and fees and expenses associated with an investment in the fund.

the index, less expenses (symbol PWC). The Dynamic Market Intel-lidex Index is rebalanced quarterly similar to many other intelligent indexes, although some are rebalanced more frequently.

Both indexes have about the same sector representation, but there are differences between their stock selection methodology. To stay timely, intelligent ETFs usually rebalance at least quarterly.

In certain periods some intelligent indexes outperform the original wave of ETFs, which are often passive indexes. Passive indexes are constructed to reflect part of an economic sector, such as the broad U.S. economy, a sector of the economy, or a geographic region any-where in the world. In other periods the original ETFs outperform intelligent ETFs.

The S&P 500 Index captures about 75 percent of the U.S. equities capitalization, and in proportion to each industry's contribution to the economy. For example, if technology comprises about 21 percent of the U.S. economy, the S&P 500 will attempt to have about a 21 per-cent weighting of technology companies in its portfolio. The S&P 500 is not prognosticating that people will make more money by holding technology stocks, but rather it is reflecting that particular industry's proportion in the U.S. economy. Intelligent indexes are different. They use methodologies to select the stocks that will be more risk averse or will outperform in the market segment they are tracking and include those stocks in their indexes.

Sometimes intelligent ETFs meet their objectives and at other times the passive ETFs perform better. Look at Figure I.2.

Figure I.2 shows the comparable performance between PWC (an intelligent ETF), DIA (the Dow Jones Industrial Average ETF), and SPY (the S&P 500 index ETF). The figure shows how the ETFs per-formed from September 2004 through August 27, 2007. PWC was up

Figure I.2

PWC, DIA, SPY Performance

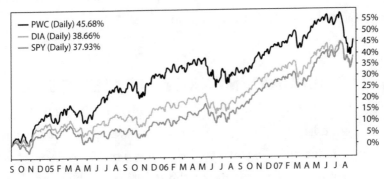

Source: Chart courtesy of StockCharts.com

about 45.6 percent in that period; DIA, up 38.6 percent; and SPY, up about 37.9 percent. This performance refers to price action and does not include dividends, fees, and other expenses.

In this period PWC (the intelligent ETF) outperformed the others, and the first-generation ETFs (DIA and SPY) performed as they were constructed to perform. DIA gave investors and traders broad market representation, and SPY gave broad U.S. economy representation with sector exposure consideration, which is what investors and traders expected of them.

The three ETFs are different in portfolio construction and stock selection methodology. PWC includes about 75 percent large-cap stocks, while DIA and SPY are essentially constructed of all large-cap stocks. There are also differences in stock selection. PWC uses its methodology to pick stocks that will outperform on the upside while attempting to give downside support. DIA attempts to represent the ups and downs of the U.S. economy in 30 stocks. SPY attempts to mirror the economy in a broader-based index, encompassing all market sectors.

It is important to learn what the various ETFs are structured to accomplish and how they structure their portfolios because this knowledge can help your investment performance.

USING ALPHA IN MARKET STRATEGIES

Look at Figure I.3, and consider it in conjunction with Table I.1. Both Figure I.3 and Table I.1 show dramatic swings in certain years.

For instance, in 1974 you would have had a bad year, losing about 29 percent buying and holding the S&P 500. If you had traded and been wrong and out of the market on the five best days, you would have been down about 42 percent, a much worse performance. But if you had been right, and missed being in the market on the five worst

Figure I.3

The Good, the Bad, and the Beautiful—Three Scenarios with a Dollar Invested

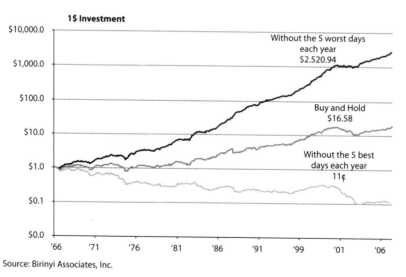

Source: Birinyi Associates, Inc.

Table I.1

Year	Annual Performance	Without 5 Best Days	Without 5 Worst Days	Year	Annual Performance	Without 5 Best Days	Without 5 Worst Days
1966	−12.86%	−21.34%	−3.27%	1987	2.03%	−20.09%	60.18%
1967	20.09	11.66	28.67	1988	12.40	−2.70	35.11
1968	7.66	−1.16	15.59	1989	27.25	14.79	43.79
1969	−11.36	−18.43	−4.08	1990	−6.56	−17.82	7.42
1970	0.10	−13.65	13.89	1991	26.31	10.05	36.74
1971	10.79	−0.06	19.40	1992	4.46	−2.95	12.60
1972	15.63	9.31	22.49	1993	7.06	−0.90	16.03
1973	−17.37	−27.23	−5.97	1994	−1.54	−9.16	7.64
1974	−29.72	−42.28	−18.06	1995	34.11	25.14	42.90
1975	31.55	18.56	45.97	1996	20.26	9.21	34.99
1976	19.15	9.83	28.70	1997	31.01	12.02	55.21
1977	−11.50	−17.30	−4.72	1998	26.67	4.52	55.96
1978	1.06	−12.63	12.88	1999	19.53	3.98	35.31
1979	12.31	2.17	24.07	2000	−10.14	−25.28	8.64
1980	25.77	11.05	43.64	2001	−13.04	−28.53	5.11
1981	−9.73	−17.24	0.99	2002	−23.37	−39.30	−7.84
1982	14.76	−5.29	30.80	2003	26.38	8.79	45.38
1983	17.27	5.12	28.89	2004	8.99	0.70	17.81
1984	1.40	−10.64	8.26	2005	3.00	−5.02	11.02
1985	26.33	15.17	34.64	2006	13.62	3.38	23.47
1986	14.62	3.41	34.30	2007*	7.73	1.06	18.21

* Through May 2007.

days, you would have been down about 18 percent, almost half as much as you would have been down buying and holding that year.

Note also the years 1987, 1988, and 2003 to see the wide returns attained by being in the market at certain times. Figure I.3 shows that to have the highest degree of success you must be in the market on the good days. However, it is very difficult to know when the good days will be.

Good traders are pretty consistent in predicting the time frames for when markets will be good or bad, but few consistently prognosticate market gyrations to the day. Usually, good traders are right 30 or 40 percent of the time and make big enough wagers so that when they *are* right they make enough to make up for the losses that are inevitably coming their way.

Spending most of your waking hours trying to outwit the market is a hard way to make a living, especially as an amateur. If you want to take some money out of the market when you think it is high, or buy when you think it is low, do this with just a portion of your portfolio. Betting it all can be rewarding, but it is also risky.

The buy and hold scenario in Figure I.3 is not as exciting as being out of the market on the five worst days, but it is better than the paltry return from missing the five best days. So in the sideways to down market that we seem to be in, it is important to stay invested. But what do you invest and trade in? This is an especially important question to consider when you are searching for alpha.

Do you buy iShares Global Sectors or the S&P 500 ETF or the SPDR series of sectors or the PowerShares FTSE RAFI 1000 companies ETF or one of the ProShares magnified ETFs or a combination of the above, and in what combination? Or should you buy another ETF? It is worth your time to understand your options.

Figure I.4 shows the comparable performances of some Power-Shares intelligent indexes against other benchmark indexes.

You could not have bought the PowerShares indexes because they were not traded in the entire periods studied. ETFs have been produced to attempt to replicate the performance of these indexes, not

Figure I.4[2]

PWC, S&P 500, Russell 3000 Performance, 1995–2007

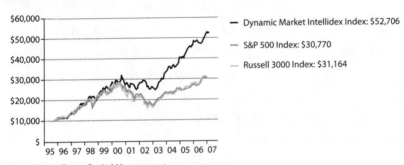

— Dynamic Market Intellidex Index: $52,706

— S&P 500 Index: $30,770

— Russell 3000 Index: $31,164

Source: PowerShares Capital Management

---

[2] Total Returns are based on the Closing Market Price. Performance data quoted represents past performance, which is not a guarantee of future results. Investment returns and principal value will fluctuate, and shares, when redeemed, may be worth more or less than their original cost. Current performance may be higher or lower than performance data quoted. After-tax returns reflect the highest federal income tax rate but exclude state and local taxes. Fund performance reflects fee waivers, absent which, performance data quoted would have been lower.

The Dynamic Market Intellidex Index return does not represent the fund return. The performance results shown are hypothetical and reflect the investment returns that might have been achieved by investing $10,000 according to the index on July 31, 1995. The results assume that no cash was added to or assets withdrawn from the hypothetical investment and that all dividends, gains, and other earnings in the account were reinvested in accordance with the index's rules. The Dynamic Market Intellidex Index does not charge management fees or brokerage expenses, and no such fees or expenses were deducted from the hypothetical performance shown. The index does not lend securities, and no revenues from securities lending were added to the performance shown. You cannot invest directly in the index. In addition, the results actual investors might have achieved would have differed from those shown because of differences in the timing, amounts of their investments, and fees and expenses associated with an investment in the fund.

counting fees and expenses. The PowerShares returns are backdated, hypothetical performances.

Figure I.4 shows that if you had invested $10,000 in the Dynamic Market Intellidex Index in July 1995, that sum would have grown to $52,706 in early 2007. That same amount invested in the S&P 500 would have grown to $30,770 over that same time. That $10,000 would have grown to $31,164 in the Russell 3000, which is a somewhat similar but broader index than the S&P 500. The Intellidex return is higher in that period than the other indexes.

PowerShares has created an ETF from the Dynamic Market Intellidex Index methodology (symbol PWC). See Figure I.5.

The calculations in Figure I.5 are again hypothetical, and you could not have invested in the time periods shown in any of the indexes included. So, hypothetically, if you had invested $10,000 in the Nasdaq 100 on January 1, 1993, you would have $50,500 in early 2007, which is about a 400 percent return. Investing that amount in the Nasdaq Composite, you would have seen your investment grow to $37,100 over the same period, a 271 percent return. The PowerShares Dynamic OTC Intellidex Index would have returned $126,262 over that same period, a return of 1,162 percent, substantially more than the other indexes.

As far as downside risk, notice that the Nasdaq 100 and the Nasdaq Composite's worth dropped to about $20,000 in the bear market of 2000 to 2003, whereas at the low point the intelligent index's worth dropped to about $50,000. This shows that an intelligent index, while outperforming in a good market, can also have downside support in a down market. The PowerShares Dynamic OTC Intellidex Index now trades as an ETF (symbol PWO).

Say you want representation in the biotech sector. You read that publicly traded biotechnology companies made over $60 billion in

Figure I.5[3]

PWO, Nasdaq Composite, Nasdaq 100 Performance, 1992–2007

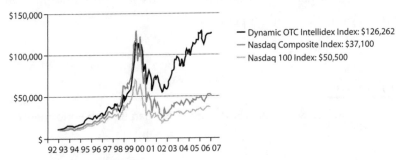

Source: PowerShares Capital Management

revenues for the first time in the sector's 30-year history (source: *Beyond Borders: The Global Biotechnology Report 2006*, Ernst & Young); that there were 32 new products approved in the United States, including 17 first-time approvals; and that globally the biotech industry raised almost $20 billion in capital in 2005, the second highest total since that market bubble burst in 2000.

---

[3] Total Returns are based on the Closing Market Price. Performance data quoted represents past performance, which is not a guarantee of future results. Investment returns and principal value will fluctuate, and shares, when redeemed, may be worth more or less than their original cost. Current performance may be higher or lower than performance data quoted. After-tax returns reflect the highest federal income tax rate but exclude state and local taxes. Fund performance reflects fee waivers, absent which, performance data quoted would have been lower.

The Dynamic OTC Intellidex Index return does not represent the fund return. The performance results shown are hypothetical and reflect the investment returns that might have been achieved by investing $10,000 according to the index on January 1, 1993. The results assume that no cash was added to or assets withdrawn from the hypothetical investment and that all dividends, gains, and other earnings in the account were reinvested in accordance with the index's rules. The Dynamic OTC Intellidex Index does not charge management fees or brokerage expenses, and no such fees or expenses were deducted from the hypothetical performance shown. The index does not lend securities, and no revenues from securities lending were added to the performance shown. You cannot invest directly in the index. In addition, the results actual investors might have achieved would have differed from those shown because of differences in the timing, amounts of their investments, and fees and expenses associated with an investment in the fund.

Although passive sector ETFs do give participation in the biotech sector's performance, you do not want passive representation. You want to gain alpha and outperform.

Consider Figure I.6.

Figure I.6[4]

Dynamic BioTech & Genome, S&P Biotech, Nasdaq Biotech Performance 2000–2007

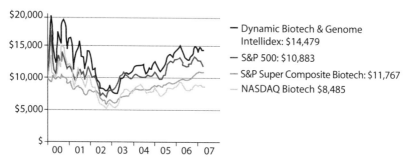

— Dynamic Biotech & Genome
Intellidex: $14,479

— S&P 500: $10,883

— S&P Super Composite Biotech: $11,767

— NASDAQ Biotech $8,485

Source: PowerShares Capital Management

[4] Total Returns are based on the Closing Market Price. Performance data quoted represents past performance, which is not a guarantee of future results. Investment returns and principal value will fluctuate, and shares, when redeemed, may be worth more or less than their original cost. Current performance may be higher or lower than performance data quoted. After-tax returns reflect the highest federal income tax rate but exclude state and local taxes. Fund performance reflects fee waivers, absent which, performance data quoted would have been lower.

The Dynamic Biotechnology & Genome Intellidex Index return does not represent the fund return. The performance results shown are hypothetical and reflect the investment returns that might have been achieved by investing $10,000 according to the index on January 1, 2000. The results assume that no cash was added to or assets withdrawn from the hypothetical investment and that all dividends, gains, and other earnings in the account were reinvested in accordance with the index's rules. The Dynamic Market Intellidex Index does not charge management fees or brokerage expenses, and no such fees or expenses were deducted from the hypothetical performance shown. The index does not lend securities, and no revenues from securities lending were added to the performance shown. You cannot invest directly in the index. In addition, the results actual investors might have achieved would have differed from those shown because of differences in the timing, amounts of their investments, and fees and expenses associated with an investment in the fund.

The calculations in Figure I.6 are hypothetical, and you could not have invested in the Dynamic Biotech & Genome Intellidex. So, hypothetically, if you had invested $10,000 in the S&P SuperComposite Biotech Index on January 1, 2000, you would have $11,767 in 2007. If you had bought the Nasdaq Biotech Index you would have $8,485. If you had bought the Dynamic Biotech & Genome Intellidex Index, which now is a PowerShares ETF (symbol PBE), you would have $14,479. The intelligent index was easily the best performer in this group.

TRADING AND INVESTING WITH ETFs

As you can see, ETFs are unique. There are as many ways to trade and invest as there are investors. Use ETFs as they fit your investing goals. If after reading this book, there is something you do not understand, e-mail me at exch13@aol.com.

Chapter | 1

EXPLAINING EXCHANGE-TRADED FUNDS

Exchange-traded funds (ETFs) are securities classes that track an index, an industry, a style group, geographic region, or other market segment, all of which is spelled out in an ETF's offering prospectus. For most ETFs that deal in stocks or bonds, this entails buying the stocks or bonds that exactly or approximately replicate its index. ETFs, especially ones of the new generation, offer exposure to stocks picked according to indexing methodologies and disciplines based on exhaustive and original research.

ETFs are constructed somewhat similar to mutual funds, but there are important differences. ETFs trade on stock exchanges like individual securities. With ETFs, investors trade a security that has even more flexibility than a stock and can gain the diversification that indexing offers.

The new generation of ETFs gives enhanced quantitative methodology that seeks to accomplish certain goals such as gaining alpha and reducing risk by diversifying. The indexes that the ETFs attempt to replicate have been back-tested and many use new weighting techniques.

For traders, during the day as the markets move up and down, you can trade ETFs as you would individual stocks, taking advantage of rallies and dips. Because you are trading a market segment, you are not subject to the high risk of trading a single issue.

For investors, you can buy a market segment or indexing methodology or any of a host of ETF offerings, hold that exposure as long as you want, for years even, and probably have a taxable event only when you sell the security. Unlike a mutual fund, there will be little or no taxable events during the time you hold it.

ADVANTAGES OF TRADING AND INVESTING IN ETFs

Investors and traders can buy and sell shares anytime the markets are open. ETFs can be bought and traded on margin; they can be sold short, and unlike stocks, which have to be shorted on an uptick, ETFs can be shorted on a downtick. Often ETFs have lower management fees than funds or active money managers. Because of the creation and redemption process, ETFs offer tax efficiencies. With ETFs you know what stocks you are getting, because you can go to the Web site of the ETF creator or other sources and see what stocks are held in the ETF.

There are also differences between buying and selling ETFs versus mutual funds. Consider Table 1.1 which shows some of the differences between the two structures.

You can see from Table 1.1 that there are advantages to trading ETFs versus mutual funds. And there are also advantages to trading ETFs versus stocks. You can buy and sell in size with ETFs and not affect the market price too much since ETFs are sold mainly on the basis of their net asset value.

TABLE 1.1

Trading Differences between ETFs and Mutual Funds

ETFs	Mutual Funds
Bought and sold throughout the day at the market price, usually close to the net asset value (NAV).	Bought and sold at the NAV; fees and expenses can be added at the end of the trading day.
Creation and redemption process, which usually creates no tax event to holders.	Redemptions can create taxable distributions for fund holders.
Portfolio holdings are constantly updated and disclosed.	Portfolio holdings are disclosed on a quarterly basis.
Options are available to trade with many ETFs.	No options available.
ETFs can be transferred between brokerage firms.	Limited transferring privileges.
No sales loads; ETFs are usually traded subject to brokerage commissions.	Sometimes charge a sales load.
Can be bought and sold like stocks, using limit orders, stop orders, and other trading specifications.	Cannot be bought and sold like stocks.
Can be traded on margin. Can be shorted and, unlike stocks, can be shorted on a downtick or zero downtick.	Cannot be bought and sold on margin. Cannot be shorted.

As mentioned, you can short an ETF on a downtick or a zero downtick, whereas a stock needs an uptick to be shorted. If a stock traded at 30 and then trades at 30.02, that price is an uptick. A stock can be shorted there. If a stock trades at 30.02 again, that second 30.02 trade would be a zero-plus tick, meaning it is continuing to trade higher. If a stock trades at 30, then at 29.95, that trade is a downtick and stock cannot be shorted there. If the next trade is again at 29.95 that is a zero downtick, and stock can still not be shorted.

This SEC rule of not shorting on a downtick or a zero downtick does not apply to ETFs. If the market is tumbling and you want to short the market to take advantage, you don't have to wait for an uptick with an ETF. This securities class is exempt from the downtick rule, and you can short in a falling market.

Say the market is looking weak and you have good gains in your portfolio and don't want to sell just now. You don't want to take the gains, which are short term and taxed at a high rate, and you think the market will still go up after a correction of 10 percent or so. You are not a trader but you do time the market on occasion. Besides, you will only short about 10 percent of your portfolio, and if you are wrong, you will be right on the 90 percent of your portfolio that you are holding.

Shorting an individual stock is generally riskier than shorting an ETF, just as buying a single stock is generally riskier than buying an ETF. ETFs are baskets of stocks, in most cases replicating stock indexes, so there is a built-in diversification component. Just like buying a stock, shorting a stock exposes you to the vicissitudes of the fortune of a single company, and the myriad unforeseen events that can affect a company at any given time. Maybe you have researched a company and know everything about it. You have great confidence in the company, most analysts praise it, and you don't see a downside, given its low P/E and low Price to Book ratio. But things happen, and you don't have to live through many Enrons and WorldComs to realize that there are limits to investment research. WorldCom looked good on paper, but in reality there were accounting problems that only surfaced after the stock had declined quite a bit.

If you want to short the market but don't know what to short, just that you want a market proxy to follow the market direction that you think is downward, you could short SPY. SPY is the symbol of one of the S&P 500 Index ETFs. Say that SPY is selling at 145.20 a share and starting to drop. As stated, with a stock you have to wait for an uptick or zero uptick, but with ETFs you can short anytime. You could call your broker and get stock protection for when you want to cover the short. You tell your broker to short 500 shares of SPY. Something as liquid as SPY can be easily short at the market. Now you have a slightly hedged position, in that just 10 percent of your portfolio is short. When shorting an ETF, you are not subject to single stock shocks. SPY will probably go in the direction of the other market indexes. You can cover the position anytime you want.

You also don't have to worry about trading size since ETFs, with the creation and redemption process, are very efficient. If there is large demand, orders for hundreds of thousands of shares, the authorized participants can create more shares. If there is too much supply, participants can redeem shares and shrink the supply. ETFs trade based on their underlying value and, to a much lesser extent, the buying and selling pressure from traders and investors throughout the day. Prices are usually kept pretty tight, but you can always put in a limit order to be sure you get the price you want.

Some ETFs have proved to be not very liquid, especially the newer and lesser known ones. But because ETFs trade on a net asset value basis, they usually do not stray far from their asset value. You do have to be careful when trading and investing in the less liquid issues. It is a good idea to watch the trading in the ETFs you are interested in and make sure they trade near their asset values.

Before I buy an ETF, especially a lesser known one, I watch the trading for a while to make sure that the trades are near the bid and asked prices. Sometimes I put in market orders to make sure that orders are executed near the bid and asked prices. When trading in a less active ETF, you could use limits on buys and sells, at least until you get comfortable enough to trust the trading in that ETF to enter market orders.

Recently I had to invest some money for a client, so I did my research and bought several ETFs. It took some time to get the trades done, but nothing like the work it would have taken to trade stocks. I bought some of the lesser known ETFs, and didn't see where I moved the market at all; in most cases I bought easily on the offered side. I could have tried to split the bid and asked, but I wanted to get the money working quickly.

Trading stocks is different, especially in the lesser known, less liquid stocks. In those cases you almost have to use limits, because without that safeguard you could make an unfortunate execution. In a fast-moving market it is often hard to get a feeling of where you can get trades done.

THE CREATION AND REDEMPTION PROCESS

ETFs are created and redeemed in *creation units*, which are blocks of ETFs, usually created in 50,000 share units. Many factors are taken into consideration in deciding to create more shares, including the need to fill orders and the desire to create more inventory. Shares are redeemed when it is decided that too many shares are outstanding and that a market can be easily made with fewer shares.

Creation and redemptions are done by *authorized participants*, which are usually large financial institutions such as banks or trust companies that have been authorized to participate in this process. Creations and redemptions are performed on a continuous basis on an ETF's net asset value (NAV). The NAV represents the total value of all the investments an ETF owns. This figure includes the value of the securities the ETF is holding, any cash components in the ETF, and any other assets, such as derivatives. When the participant delivers the basket of shares to be converted into ETF shares, it also brings cash to cover items such as accrued dividends, creation fees, and interest on dividends. The NAV reflects the value of the ETF shares, and ETF market prices fluctuate during the day due to supply and demand. Factors that change the NAV during the trading day include currency exchange rate fluctuations and changes in the value of the securities in the index.

Investors and traders can see the approximate value of an ETF by checking its intra-day portfolio value (IPV). Although an ETF NAV is set once a day, the IPV constantly changes throughout the trading day. The IPV does not reflect at what price an ETF can be created or redeemed, but it is an indication of the value of the stocks comprising the index. When buying or trading ETFs, the ETF market price is a moving target, similar to stock prices. However, ETFs are usually less volatile because they are baskets of stocks. When you buy a fast-moving tech stock, you know that in falling markets you may buy it cheaper and in rising markets you may have to pay up from its last price. This is true of ETFs also. When oil stocks are running, you usually have to pay up for an energy ETF.

There are instances where the IPV is not tied to the value of the underlying stocks but is more an indication of prices. One example is trading and investing in the ETFs of foreign countries and regions. Some of these ETFs are trading on the U.S. markets and are Asian,

European, or other foreign ETFs. Asia and Europe are sleeping during our trading days, and those markets are closed. The IPV in this circumstance is an indication *only*; an indication of where traders and investors in the United States think those ETFs will trade. Even so, foreign ETFs have a good record of keeping fairly close approximate prices to the actual prices of stocks in the foreign regions. Traders and investors can usually get the IPV symbol for an ETF from the ETF prospectus or the ETF creator's Web site.

For most ETFs the creation process includes buying all the stocks that comprise the index the ETF is attempting to emulate. There are also ETFs that optimize an index, meaning that the shares are not held in the exact proportion in which the replicated index holds the shares. The ETF maker describes in the prospectus whether the ETF optimizes or uses other methods for construction. Also the prospectus will reveal if and to what extent derivatives and other instruments are used.

Authorized participants calculate the number of shares of each stock needed to replicate an index. The participants tell the specialist the number of shares needed to buy to create a basket of stocks to comprise the index. As an example, consider two of the ETFs that replicate the S&P 500 Index, which are SPY and IVV. The specialist will be told what shares to buy to replicate 50,000 shares of this index: perhaps 345 shares of IBM, 180 shares of Wal-Mart, and so on. This basket of shares will be presented to authorized participants, accompanied by a cash component to cover items such as creation fees, accrued dividends, interest on dividends, any capital gains less losses that have not been reinvested since the last distribution, and usually a small amount to cover differences resulting from the rounding of the number of shares that need to be delivered.

In the ETF creation and redemption structure the money flows from the buyer to the broker, through the ETF market maker, to the ETF creator. The ETF creator creates the ETF shares, flows them through the ETF market maker, and back to the buyer. Most ETFs are created this way and most ETFs are backed by shares of stock. In the mutual fund structure the cash flows from the buyer to the fund, the fund buys shares in the capital markets, and flows fund shares back to the buyer.

So when you buy a fund, you buy from the fund itself, and the fund goes into the capital markets to buy shares. When you buy an ETF, you buy from the ETF market maker. When ETF shares are redeemed they are redeemed in kind, which benefits you and is not a tax event.

For ETF creation, when the authorized participant requests the basket of stocks, the specialist on the floor of the exchange will deliver the shares, which were bought on the open market. The participating firm can deliver the new ETFs to the specialist. As the value of the replicated index fluctuates that day, the new ETFs will trade in the open market. The key to this process is that the transaction between the specialist and the participating member happens *in kind*. The specialist on the floor does not deliver cash; the basket of stocks is delivered to the participant. The participant delivers new ETF shares. This creates no or very little tax consequence for you, the ETF buyer.

TAX CONSIDERATIONS

You do not know your potential tax liability when you buy a mutual fund. Mutual fund shares are purchased and redeemed from the fund itself, and when the fund needs cash to pay its shareholders who are redeeming shares, it may incur a capital gain that will be paid by those who have held or still hold the fund. A phantom capital gain is not a welcome surprise, especially if you sold the stock at a loss and get taxed for a gain. With ETFs this threat is minimized.

Suppose a fund has grown over many years, and the stock the fund holds has increased in price, and the cost basis of the shares in the fund is well below the NAV of the fund. For example, suppose the market price of the fund is $10 a share and its NAV is also $10 a share. The cost basis of the stock in this case averages about $5. There would be a built-in short- and/or long-term gain in the fund's market price.

If owners of the fund sell their shares, for example, when tech holders started selling shares in the tech implosion starting in 2002, the fund would have to sell stock to redeem its fund holders. The fund could decide to sell off their lowest-cost stock, not an unusual decision since this would be stock held the longest, and probably would qualify for capital-gains tax status. These capital gains would be passed on to fund holders when a capital-gains distribution is made at year end. So even if a fund holder bought and held the fund and did no other trading, she could find herself facing a taxable event because she received a capital-gains distribution.

Because of the ETF creation and redemption process, an investor or trader buys shares on an exchange. This is unlike buying a fund, because a fund buyer buys directly from the fund. Of course, there will be tax consequences when taking a profit or loss from the purchase and sale of ETFs, but only when the shares are sold or, in the case of short-ing, when the positions are covered.

Another example may clarify what could happen and the differences between funds and ETFs. Let's say that a new fund is created and the price is $100 a share. Your friend buys it and the fund goes up. He tells you about it and you buy, paying $200 a share. After that the market goes down and holders start selling the fund. The fund would have to sell shares to pay redeeming fund holders. When the fund sells its low-cost shares, it has to take a capital gain, in this case $25 a share. You hold your shares and the stock goes down to $100 a share.

What about the capital gains the fund had to take? It will be dis-tributed, and the distribution goes out to all the fund holders, includ-ing you. You would receive a capital-gains distribution of $25 a share, on which you must pay taxes, even though your shares have declined by half. The net result is that you have a $100 loss in the market value of your fund.

The above example does happen. Market cycles come and go, and funds go up in value, and when the sector or market segment the fund specializes in falls out of favor, and the fund declines, fund holders will redeem their shares, and whatever capital gains there are will be passed on to the fund holders. The conventional fund structure is part of the problem of phantom gains appearing for an investor holding a losing fund. Another possibility that could cause a mutual fund to incur large capital gains that it would have to pass on to investors has to do with the merger and corporate finance activities that have increased with the global economy. A fund could have low-cost shares of a major indus-trial company, which the fund does not plan to sell in the foreseeable future. Another company could come along, a company headquartered anywhere in the world, and take over the company in which the fund has low-priced shares. With the takeover the fund will incur a capital gain and, of course, pass the gain on to the fund holders.

ETFs AND MUTUAL FUND TAX CONSEQUENCES

In a way ETFs allow traders and investors to determine when they have to pay taxes. If an ETF has a history of paying no or very little capital gains, an investor or trader can buy or trade in the ETF and have a taxable event only when the ETF is sold. In a mutual fund the fund holders determine when all the holders have a taxable event. This is because a taxable event occurs when holders redeem their shares, forcing the fund to sell stock to pay the redemptions. This forced liquidation creates a taxable event, either a capital gain or capital loss.

MARKET MAKERS AND SPECIALISTS

ETF share prices should not get that far away from their NAV value because of trading activity on the exchanges. In over-the-counter (OTC) markets, people who are ready to buy or sell at their publicly quoted bid or asked prices are *market makers*. People who fulfill this function on the exchanges, which operate as auction markets, are charged with maintaining a fair and orderly market, and are called *specialists*.

The specialist is charged with all the functions necessary to create a fair and orderly market. Specialists are located on the floors of the exchanges, such as the American Stock Exchange (AMEX) or the

New York Stock Exchange (NYSE). Surrounding the specialists are brokers who buy and sell ETFs throughout the day. This trading market usually keeps ETF prices near their IPV. Brokers know what the IPV is and the market price and will buy or sell an ETF if and when differences widen between these two prices.

For example, if the IPV on SPY, the Standard & Poor's 500 Index, was $142 and the ETF was selling at $141.50, brokers could buy the shares, calculating that the ETF would rise to its IPV. If SPY's IPV was $142 and the ETF was selling at $142.50, brokers and traders would sell into the market, taking a profit.

This trading crowd could also arbitrage price differences. Arbitrage means buying a security in one market and selling it or a replicating derivative of it in another market, locking in the profit. For instance, if SPY were cheap in comparison to the S&P 500 Index future, the market crowd could buy SPY and sell the future, locking in a profit.

There are many strategies that traders and brokers use to arbitrage. The point is that market activity on the floor will keep ETF share prices tight because these market participants can make money exploiting the differences in the market value and the market price of the ETFs.

HARVESTING TAX LOSSES USING ETFs

ETFs are efficient in helping market participants who want to take tax losses and still do not want to lose their investment position.

Say you have stock losses that you want to take, but you think the market segment that you have losses in will do well and you do not want to lose that position. Say your portfolio is heavy in tech shares and you have a large position in Intel. The sector has done well recently, but you have losses from shares you bought in 2000, when the sector was selling at breathtaking highs. You like the sector, want to stay in it, but can use the loss against gains you have taken.

Under tax regulations, if you buy the same or similar stock shortly after the sale or shortly before the sale you cannot deduct your loss for tax purposes. There is a *wash sale provision* specifying that if you sell stock at a loss and buy substantially identical securities within 30 days before or after the sale, you will suffer an adverse tax consequence.

For example, on July 30 you sell Intel at a loss. On August 11 you buy Intel back. The sale on July 30 is a *wash sale*. The wash sale period for any sale at a loss consists of 61 calendar days, and includes the day of the sale, the 30 days before the sale, and the 30 days after the sale. The general rule is that if you are taking a deduction, you cannot purchase the same, or substantially the same, stock during the wash sale period.

None of the information in this book is meant as tax advice; for that you should see a tax attorney or a certified public accountant (CPA). Every case is different, and this general information is meant to make you aware of your options, not to advise you of your tax situation or remedies.

In the Intel example, what you *could* do is sell your Intel shares and buy an ETF that is in the same sector as Intel, expecting that the sector ETF will go in the same direction as Intel. Studies have shown that sector selection is the most important factor in making money in the market, and that stocks in a sector tend to go in the same direction. You could sell Intel and buy IYW, which is the iShare Dow Jones U.S. Technology Sector ETF. That sector includes a 6.56 weighting in Intel, and contains other large U.S. technology companies.

After you trade you will still have representation in technology and have taken a tax loss. You can wait 31 days and sell IYW and buy back Intel if that is your wish. Note that the Internal Revenue Service has not clearly defined "substantially identical" securities, nor has it clarified its interpretation of the wash sale rules and ETFs.

Chapter | 2

INVESTING IN A RAPIDLY CHANGING WORLD

Money managers have to stay ahead of the curve, anticipating which sectors, countries, cap sizes, and other market niches will do well and which will suffer, putting investment capital where the profits will be relatively highest. There are so many factors at work that anticipating future performance requires both art and science.

Getting out of markets and waiting for a good time to buy can be a losing game. So if a manager is mostly fully invested she must constantly review portfolios to see that the holdings reflect her outlook.

I have a bull bias, since capitalism and the markets essentially reflect the aspirations of people. People will usually find a way to survive and also to prosper, and capitalism gives people a way to accomplish their dreams.

The history of growing global capitalism is established, and it is hard to be negative. Besides, being negative can cost you money. So I do my research and also turn to economists and other professionals to help me figure out what is "going on out there."

GAVEKAL'S VIEW

GaveKal Research is constantly observing what is happening in the global economy, and its research attempts to stay ahead of the curve. Headquartered in Hong Kong, the firm focuses on macroeconomics and tactical asset allocation for institutional clients around the world. GaveKal posits that we are living in times of an accelerating pace of innovation, that this pace will continue, and that this is what is driving the global economy.

The firm alleges that the "Prophets of Doom"—those politicians, economists, and other experts who have continued to predict a day of reckoning for years—are usually very vociferous. The gloomy predictors say this reckoning will be atonement for past years of consumption overindulgence, borrowing, and speculating. The gloomy predictors have been wrong since the mid-1980s, although some fears have proved well-founded lately. Every year they warn about the terrifying instability of the world economy. And as the global economy has grown, they have explained away why they were wrong and why their predicted catastrophe did not happen. Often the predictors blame the financial or political manipulations on one economic or political party or another. Then they say, dire consequences have only been postponed; they will happen soon; and the results will be even more horrific.

GaveKal believes that doomsday predictors misunderstand that a liberal, competitive economy encourages billions of intelligent and motivated people worldwide to overcome economic challenges.

Time is on the side of stability in a competitive global economy. It is a positive action for governments to refrain from problem solving and let the problems work themselves out. In the United States, for example, the government has not tried to solve the trade deficits or the low rate of savings by U.S. households that the gloom and doom predictors are claiming will lead to a catastrophe.

GaveKal thinks in a liberal, competitive economy, a perceived problem that is not being solved by government is not necessarily being magnified. They and other economists admit they do not understand the implications of the many changes in the global economic scene, but they do understand that there are changes affecting past understanding of economic measures. The way GaveKal sees it, powerful forces have been in effect in the global economy since the early 1990s.

The collapse of communism has given about 3 billion new consumers and producers the opportunity to participate in the benefits of capitalism. Free trade has spread globally, allowing these new capitalists to engage in free enterprise for the first time. Technology advances have cut communication and information costs drastically, while creating a global connectivity that was never available before, certainly not at the level it is today. Financial advances have spread worldwide, giving consumers the freedom to manage their assets and liabilities, a freedom previously available only to large global companies. Central banks in various countries have upgraded their policies, allowing countries to grow in long-term productive trends. These changes have actually made the global economy more stable than ever before.

The shift of many manufacturing functions from the United States to China, for example, has created huge trade imbalances that favor China. The globalization process has made these imbalances easier to finance. The shift away from manufacturing in the United States and other developed countries into more growth in their services sectors has made the economies of the developed countries more stable than ever. Households can borrow more freely since financial services are now global, and it is easier to get the flow of capital to where it is needed. This makes the economies of the developed countries even more stable.

WHAT REVOLUTION ARE WE IN?

We are witnessing exciting times on a global scale, even though they can look confusing and perilous. The first revolution was the industrial revolution, and it multiplied what a person could do physically by using machines in place of an individual's personal strength. We are now in a technological revolution that is multiplying a person's intellectual strength. Information can be received or sent across the globe with a click. Businesses can expand no matter where in the world they are located. This allows for a worldwide integration of manufacturing where it can be done in the cheapest, most efficient way.

The present-day financial revolution involves the movement of money across borders and oceans. Global mergers and acquisitions, company buyouts across country borders, and multiple stock listings on exchanges across the globe are part of the developments making money available to consumers and businesses like never before.

The health care revolution is here because people are living longer, healthier, and more productive lives. The advances of multinational pharmaceutical firms and the results of years of biotech research are having profound effects on the health of people around the globe.

In this revolution, markets are emerging with many of their problems of the past resolved or brought under control. Instead of worrying about the next harvest, and fearing that a famine might wipe out large numbers of the population, emerging countries are turning to endeavors such as manufacturing, services, and technological activities that are making it possible for large numbers of their people to enjoy a high standard of living, instead of just a privileged few.

Another revolution is a lifestyle revolution caused by a continuously shrinking percentage of income spent on essentials like food and clothing, and more income spent on things such as leisure, entertainment, and high-end merchandise. This is evident by the fact that high-end priced items, such as autos, luxury apartments, and clothing, are the most in demand. In fact, we hear that it has never been so expensive to be rich, with prices for high-end items advancing because of strong demand.

Lastly there is a revolution in the corporate business model and the global integration that allows businesses and nations to do what they do most efficiently, leading to new savings and growth.

THE "PLATFORM" OPERATING MODEL

The new operating model for corporations in advanced countries, such as the United States, Sweden, the United Kingdom, and Germany, is creating a deflationary boom that could last for decades.

GaveKal's theory, which focuses on why global economies are expanding, is that the platform operating model allows companies to focus on performing those functions which allow them to add the most value. This includes using knowledge, technology, and information communications to enhance their platform operational model. The platform approach allows a company to do those things that the company does best, and outsource what it doesn't do as well or doesn't do economically. In this way the company is outsourcing the more volatile and inefficient parts of its business.

One example of this is Nike, a corporation with ideas, marketing methods, while global inventory controls that are the brains of its operation, while the brawn is in the manufacturing aspect. Manufacturing can be done anywhere in the world, wherever the costs are lowest, and Nike does not have a competitive edge in the manufacturing function.

Instead of being a running shoe, apparel, and sports equipment company, Nike is more of a marketing and research technology company, sometimes acting as a sort of middleman between its customers and the worldwide plants that manufacture its products and use the Nike name.

This arrangement does not have to sacrifice quality; in fact, there is a point of view that Nike enhances quality by outsourcing its manufacturing function to those manufacturers who do this function the best. By using its brains and computers, Nike can service its customers well, ensure that its manufacturers build in quality, and that its customers will receive cutting-edge, quality merchandise.

It is unlikely that Nike and the other Western-world platform companies could produce products as cheaply as they do and of such high quality if they didn't operate under a platform company structure.

Another example of a platform company is Starbucks, a company that serves coffee day and night around the world, but grows no coffee, owns no coffee plantations, and has no managers who go out into the field and get their hands dirty planting coffee seeds. Starbucks sells coffee drinkers a wide selection of coffees from around the globe. Its coffee buyers are out in the field selecting coffees from everywhere. They travel to the coffee-growing regions of Latin America, Asia, Arabia, and elsewhere, and select the finest beans. Starbucks uses its own methods to roast the beans. It then sells its coffee to customers, offering combinations of drinks and ingredients in many varieties. It could be said that Starbucks is selling choices, and this is obviously what people want, because the company keeps growing. They also make good coffee.

Imagine if Starbucks planted the seeds, grew its own coffee, negotiated with local governments all over the world for permits, hired workers to plant seeds, oversaw the workers, and figured out which workers were not working efficiently and fired them, dealt with unions, and all the other things managers must do. This is not what Starbucks does best. The company uses its brains, technology, and experience to determine what its customers want and then finds a way to cheaply and efficiently fill their orders. Creating needs by creating variety is the value that Starbucks adds, and it fills a niche that it created for itself.

Starbucks has created a brand that is connected with the consumer, and it is monetizing its intangible asset—its brand name—to be able to charge a premium amount for a cup of coffee and other products. As a retail platform company, Starbucks can monetize other avenues in its retail space. For instance, Starbucks has opened up a line of music sales and other products, all sales taking place in its retail stores. The company has figured out how to allocate its capital, its tasks, and build a brand, all steps necessary to create a large reservoir of intellectual capital, and they have expanded into the broad world to monetize this reservoir most fully.

Another trend that Starbucks is bringing into the world is mass customization. In the industrial age, people would buy the same common product from a company. But Starbucks offers all sorts of coffee drinks. It has been estimated that if all the combinations of drinks that can be bought at Starbucks, including the different sizes and different flavors and different milk ingredients, were counted up, the number would be in the hundreds of thousands or even millions. This makes Starbucks a mass marketer of customized product.

Starbucks sells a good cup of coffee but has developed this theme into a mass customized product. This plays into the global trend of determining what consumers want and then delivering this product to them cheaply and efficiently. If Starbucks, for instance, announced that it would only sell a medium-sized latte, and make it only with nonfat milk, that would make for a limited amount of sales because it would be selling only one product. Because it customizes its coffee menu, Starbucks has created a million or so different products it can sell. Also, there are very little or no marginal costs to offer this great variety.

As far as offering products other than coffee, the reason that Starbucks and similar companies can expand their product lines is explained in part by "The Long Tail" theory of economics, as expounded by Chris Anderson, author of *The Long Tail: Why the Future of Business Is Selling Less of More* (Hyperion, 2006).

Anderson writes that we don't all watch the same television shows, listen to the same news stations, and otherwise function as we once did in the past. It used to be that Wal-Mart and Sears were the main places we could shop. We now have many alternative places to shop, stations to watch or listen to, and many sites on the Internet to help us choose our products and services.

The presence of many niche sources, especially those found on the Internet, has created a whole new place for people to find merchandise they want. With Web sites offering thousands of radio stations and Amazon.com selling books that are almost impossible to find in bookstores, the choices for consumers are almost infinite. The idea is, if you can sell a small amount of hard-to-find items to a large amount of people, you have a good market.

This long tail is applicable to Starbucks and the music placed in its stores, music that you might not find in other places, or that is hard to find. Market surveys show that certain music fits the Starbucks customer profile, and that is what is placed in their retail stores. Starbucks also sells coffee filters, coffeemakers, and all sorts of products that might be hard to find or have a limited consumer need. These products can be sold in volume in their retail outlets because they are what the typical Starbucks customer could be looking for.

Platform retail companies can succeed globally, but it is not easy for them to fully monetize their intellectual capital. The same module that works for a company in the United States, for example, may not work in other countries, or may not work at certain times.

For instance, Wal-Mart has been a huge success in the United States, Mexico, and other countries. But in early 2007 the company left South Korea, announcing that it could not figure out the South Korean market satisfactorily enough to continue its operations there. Many companies that have been very successful in some foreign nations have pulled out of other countries where their model did not work, for whatever reason.

The United States and other developed countries have many Nike and Starbucks stores, and the list is growing. They represent companies that employ methods born of ideas that return high bottom-line margins, where inventory controls are aided by a large and growing technology component, and where manufacturing is outsourced wherever it can be done the cheapest and most efficiently. The work of manufacturing is also becoming more efficient and streamlined.

Some economists such as GaveKal believe that this global platform model is taking the wide economic cycles out of the global economy.

Because the platform model is different and its usage is larger, it is necessary to look at the way economic factors have been measured in the past. The large and growing U.S. trade deficit and the low U.S. household savings rate may not be problems or may not be symptomatic of underlying problems. In fact, they may be positive results of a robust global economy. For instance, the mortgage, credit card, and auto debt delinquency rate has declined from 6 percent in the early 1990s to between 1.5 and 2.5 percent recently (Source, Reuters EcoWin). This is at a time when U.S. consumers have been increasing their household debt.

Global platform corporations are experiencing growing after-tax profits and gross after-tax cash flow, leading to a stable rate of change in industrial production. These factors have also led to a low and stable interest rate environment.

THE GROWING U.S. STRENGTH USING THE PLATFORM MODEL

Whether making and exporting items such as beer, soup, jet engines, or all sorts of services to anywhere in the world, U.S. companies are in a position to monetize these items desired and needed by worldwide consumers. The margins for its products are very good for U.S. companies.

For instance, an iPod could be made in Singapore and be sold to a person in China, Poland, Argentina, or anywhere in the world. Apple Computer, Inc. receives a royalty for the production of that iPod. The 10 million iPods sold after the first one, and the 10 million after that, and so on, bring in marginal revenue for Apple (the U.S. company that owns the intellectual property), and Apple's costs are marginal to receive this income stream.

For some idea of how important U.S. products are to a country, consider that through U.S. operating affiliates, the United States accounts for about 13 percent of the Singapore GDP, which is a large amount. This income stream from intellectual properties also applies to makers of U.S. movies and pharmaceutical, technological, biotech, and other products.

Platform companies know that the design and distribution of their products are where they can add value, and the manufacturing of the product is really not where value is added. A platform company will move the production of its product to an overseas locale such as China or the Czech Republic, where it can be done cheaply and well, but keep the design and distribution of that product as its own function. The conception, design, and distribution of a product are where the margins are the highest.

THE PRESENT ECONOMIC AGE

Today there is a different way to look at economics. In the industrial age, economics was always about the allocation of scarce resources.

When considering knowledge, the input of knowledge, and knowledge as a capital base that companies use to create earnings, knowledge is fundamentally different in many ways than labor. From a physical capital input, the way to look at economics is no longer the study of the allocation of scarce resources, but as the allocation of abundant resources.

When you combine these ideas, what you see is a world comprised of nations performing different product-development functions and continuing to move up a value chain. For instance, 10 years from now China will not be making basic items like T-shirts and Christmas ornaments. That function will have moved to Vietnam or Bangladesh, or other more economically remote areas. Every country is moving up the value chain, and that is the happy ending for the present economic global reality. To the extent that this global separation of tasks is allowed to play out, it is the natural progression of every nation to continue to move up the value chain to a higher function—and that includes the United States.

This global working method is creating a production mode where the whole is worth more than the sum of the parts. In this way pieces of the global economy make the entire global output worth more than every single piece of the economy that created the whole. This is not to say that this development is orderly or even assured. Bad monetary policy, bad fiscal policy, protectionism, increasing taxes, and war are some of the disruptive forces that could cause global financial problems. It does not appear that any of these factors are ready to derail the massive globalization process that has developed and is growing, or the benefits that this process is bringing.

TYPES OF DEVELOPING GROWTH

It is hard to understand the developing world's economic growth today because there are different types of growth developing, sometimes all at the same time. This one is perhaps different from any other time in history.

RICARDIAN ECONOMICS

Ricardian economics is alive and working in the world today. These theories are attributed to David Ricardo, an economist born in 1772. Ricardo espoused his idea known as the theory of comparative advantage, which is that one country may have the ability to produce goods cheaper than another country. The country that produces goods at a higher price may have other abilities, and should therefore exploit those abilities, allowing the lower-cost country to fulfill its advantageous function.

Ricardo was opposed to tariffs between nations and advocated perfect competition and undistorted markets, thinking that would lead to countries exporting products in which they had comparative advantages.

This is the type of growth that has been developed between the United States, other Western developed nations, China, Asia, and the rest of the world. Manufacturing capabilities are being relocated from the West to Asia and other lesser developed regions. According to the Ricardian theory, China and other regions are better at manufacturing than the United States and other developed countries. The developed countries are better at product development and marketing. It follows that the United States and similar countries should develop products, market them, and outsource the manufacturing component, which is exactly what has happened. This Ricardian growth has been a huge factor in increasing global exchange. This growth has helped the United States and other developed economies as well as the emerging markets around the globe.

This type of growth started years ago, even before the Berlin Wall was torn down. Since the wall came down in 1989, a good portion of the world's population has moved to a capitalist economy. But global growth began before that event. In the 1800s, growth in world trade exploded when countries started moving from agrarian to industrial societies. In the United States, this move from an agrarian to an industrial society was very difficult, as it was in the rest of the world. The Civil War was partly a struggle between the rapidly industrializing North and the slowly industrializing South. These regions were coming to grips with how to function in their new society.

In the 1800s, large portions of Europe also had a difficult time transitioning from an agrarian to an industrial society. Two world wars in Europe were due at least in part to this difficult transition. Similarly, in Asia, Mao Tse-tung's movement to take over China in 1949 was partly an economic revolution. The movement transformed China into a major power that is now a capitalist system.

Charles Gave, chairman of GaveKal Research believes there has been a return to a capitalist deflationary trend over the last 20 years or so. More people are rejoining the capitalist community and producing ever more value as they do so. This leads him to the conclusion that the highly developed economies of the United States, Japan, and other developed countries are exporting their new product models to be manufactured in underdeveloped countries in Asia, Eastern Europe, South America, and other regions. This is a Ricardian-type model growth.

In this Ricardian growth development, the underdeveloped countries are rebuilding their manufacturing facilities. This rebuilding is allowing new entrants into the global marketplace to participate in activities in which the developed nations no longer have a comparative advantage. This includes the manufacturing of products such as cars, television sets, and electronic items.

Outsourcing the manufacturing process to countries that have a competitive advantage frees up resources, land, labor, and capital, allowing these developing countries to use their resources in more value-added growth opportunities. These higher-value opportunities could be activities such as decoding the human genome, further breakthroughs in information technology, and involvement in the explosion of new products in the financial services industry.

Along with this Ricardian growth in the developed countries, there is Schumpeterian growth. The combination of these two factors is causing a dynamic state of change.

SCHUMPETERIAN ECONOMICS

Schumpeterian economics describes a type of economic growth that is based on the process of creative destruction. This process was described by Joseph Schumpeter in his writings and refers to the introduction of new products and new processes that are constantly being developed. Capitalism is an evolutionary process, Schumpeter wrote, and with capitalism comes an impulse to make things better, cheaper, or more usable and therefore more profitable. With recent technological tools, this creative destruction seems to be moving faster than ever.

As an example, when the fax machine came out, it replaced the telex machine. When the e-mail function was developed, it replaced the fax machine or certainly diminished its use.

In this twofold growth global dynamic then, there is outsourcing to those countries that do the most efficient job in manufacturing. Inside the developed countries with their corporate platform operations, there is Schumpeterian destructive capitalism, causing great efficiencies and savings. These factors are causing an overlaying in breadth and depth of competitive pressures, which are creating the usage of a very efficient allocation of resources.

This convergence of Schumpeterian and Ricardian growth has aided the development of globalization. No longer do the individual inputs of production need to be in a centralized location. Resources can be extracted from the ground in one part of the world and sent halfway around the world for processing or other labor input, and then sent back halfway around the world for its ultimate consumption destination. Globalization in many ways has made intellectual improvements in the production process. This economic development and growth has been hard for market investors and traders and the general public to understand. Many people regard this growth as unsustainable for a variety of reasons. Along with the economic integration of nations, there is a greater financial integration of nations.

THE NEW GLOBAL MANUFACTURING PROCESS

Globally there are two overriding forces: the allocation of capital and the allocation of task.

The factors of production have become separated, and now every company doesn't need to have a manufacturing plant or means of production. It is not necessary for companies to have raw materials coming in the back door, the labor in place to handle it, and a completed car, as an example, coming out the front door. This was the model of the car manufacturers in the 1930s and 1940s. This model was shared by all the corporations of that time as a basic means of production.

The factors of production are separated today, allowing the factors of manufacturing to specialize in the areas that they do well. Businesses can now invest their capital on their high-margin operations and not have to spread it around to the lower-margin aspects of their operations. A company can look at everything it does and calculate whether it has a comparative advantage in its activities or if it would be better off outsourcing as part of its manufacturing process. This would allow it to focus on the design or another aspect of its corporate process.

As an example, a company may have a three-part step in its manufacturing process. The company may realize that it does not have a competitive advantage in two, or even three, of the manufacturing steps. The company realizes it can find manufacturers anywhere in the world. Given the Ricardian growth era we are in, manufacturers can add value by the quality of their production capabilities. The company decides to find a manufacturer and outsource the manufacturing job. The company will simply use its intellectual properties to design the ultimate products, infuse those products with the company's intellectual property, and farm out the manufacturing to a company that can add value.

THE HIGH MARGINS OF THE PLATFORM METHOD

Returning to our example of the Apple iPod, we see that the parts for the iPod are made all over Asia, yet the ultimate consumer in many instances is in the United States and Europe. From this product Apple earns the highest return of all the participants in the manufacturing process. Considering all the value-added features of each function, the preponderance of the added value is done by Apple for designing and distributing its product.

As far as capital and its role in these processes, more industrial companies, especially in the United States, have gotten more into the business of allocating tasks, including allocating capital.

To the extent that the United States moves up the value chain and continues to be a leader in global growth, U.S. companies will become more involved in the allocation of its capital; therefore, the allocation of its task becomes greater. The United States, despite all the complications it faces in the global marketplace, is analogous to a commercial bank. A bank takes in capital and pays its depositors 4 or 5 percent to use their capital. The bank invests that money at 7 or 8 percent and takes the spread as a profit. That's the dominant U.S. corporate business model.

The global economy allows all nations to rise up the value chain. Though there are risks and challenges, this development is a positive force driving the future of global trade.

LOWER STOCK MARKET AND GDP VOLATILITY

The platform model structure makes it necessary to look at the United States and foreign stock markets in a fresh way. Since information

Figure 2.1

Quarterly Volatility of U.S. GDP

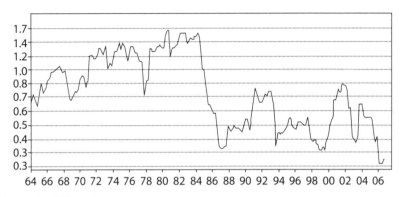

Source: GaveKal Research

technology (IT) is such an important and growing factor in the model, this sector should continue to grow. The growing usage of the platform operational model and the innovative use of IT seem to have taken the wide cycles out of the global economy and have helped create lower interest rates. The drop in the volatility of the U.S. gross domestic product (GDP) seems to confirm this belief. From 1964 to 1984, the U.S. economy grew at a 3 percent rate, with a high volatility in its quarterly growth rate. Since 1984 the GDP has continued to grow at a 3 percent rate, but its volatility has dropped sharply. See Figure 2.1.

Along with a drop in GDP volatility, there has been a drop in stock market volatility. The volatility index (VIX) measures the volatility of the S&P 500 Index. VIX dropped from a high of 21 in March 2007 to a low of 13 in April 2007. This drop in volatility has been going on for some time. In March 2003 the VIX was at the 36 level, and has trended lower since that time.

This lower economic volatility could continue and, if so, would give households around the world, especially in the Western developed nations where the platform companies are located, more stability and less risk from an uncertain economic cycle. Also, stock market volatility could stay lower. Lower volatility is one of the many new developments occurring in the global economy. This is not reported on the evening news or in newspapers and is not generally recognized. The low savings rate and the balance-of-payments deficit in the United States are seldom mentioned except in the worst terms, as signs that the United States is deteriorating.

THE LOWER U.S. HOUSEHOLD SAVINGS RATE

Most economists like to point out how the U.S. household inflation rate has dropped and continues to be low, and how this is a sign of profligacy, potentially bad economic conditions for families, and a general decline in our national well-being. Households that have low savings rates have been tied to a general moral degeneration, along with all sorts of other ills.

But if we *are* in a more developed economy than ever before, it is contended that there might be good reasons for low household savings rates.

There are opinions that savings rates are calculated only as income derived from work and do not include capital gains. The growth in value of stocks, houses, and other assets is not included in a household's savings rate. It deducts from work income all expenses, including house maintenance expenses and also capital gains taxes. In many ways this method of measuring the savings rate is not applicable to the real-world setup of how households in the Western developed nations, like the United States, operate. For many people in these countries, income from capital gains, especially in the higher-income households, can be higher than income derived from work.

Money held by Americans *is* growing. In its book *The End Is Not Nigh*, GaveKal Research reports that in the year 2005 Americans contributed $650 billion to U.S. savings classes such as equity and bond funds. Americans also had over $5.3 trillion in money-market funds, certificates of deposit (CDs), and savings accounts, which was up from $4.9 trillion in 2004.

The question could be asked: Why are household savings rates so important? Why do economists attach such importance to it, even to the point of claiming that it is almost sinful to have a low savings rate. Yes, it is evident that saving for a rainy day is important. Also, saving for when one can no longer work and has to live off the fruits of one's labor makes sense. But today there are new realities to be considered. Perhaps economic thinking and planning should be done differently because we are in the time of the platform operating companies and an open global trade era.

In Figure 2.1 we see that economic volatility has been reduced. The United States has evolved into more of a service economy than a hard labor economy, with farming and manufacturing labor comprising less of GDP. A switch to jobs that are less physical means that people can work longer and may not have to worry as much about a time when they can no longer work. This lower volatility helps both corporations and households and makes it less critical to have high savings as backup funds.

When economic cycles are fairly tame, companies can borrow more. This is because banks are more certain that their loans will be repaid. Banks are risk averse and do not like wide economic cycle highs and lows because the low cycles put them at risk. Companies may go bust and not be able to pay back their borrowed funds. It is the same with personal loans. When people are at risk because they may lose their jobs, lenders are less likely to lend them money, or may lend them less money.

When companies and households can tap lenders easily, they have less need to have high rates of savings. And with savings funds freed up, they can invest these funds in real estate, securities, and other items that will grow for them in the future.

THE U.S. BALANCE-OF-TRADE DEFICIT

One reason that the United States runs a current trade deficit is because global growth is moving from the developed economies to the emerging market companies. With 3 billion new capitalists joining the trading system, this would be a logical development.

The current account numbers have to do with trade but not with profitability. The Western nations' platform company model returns the most profit to the developed countries, as a result of their marketing and technology function. The manufacturing function that is outsourced, mostly to emerging countries, receives the lower profit end of the process.

GaveKal's statistics show, for instance, that when Dell ships a $500 computer manufactured in China to a customer in the United States, this is calculated as an import from China. Dell's profit from this sale would be about $200, whereas the Chinese company that manufactured the computer would keep about $50.

Production costs are registered in official figures, whereas profits and the value added are not. This may be an important factor in whether the U.S. current account deficit is accurate or meaningful. In fact, this could mean that the United States is not borrowing the huge reported numbers from other countries. This would explain why

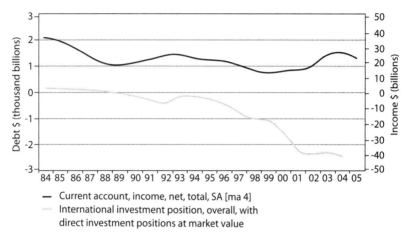

U.S. Net Foreign Debt and Net Foreign Investment Income

— Current account, income, net, total, SA [ma 4]
— International investment position, overall, with
  direct investment positions at market value

Source: GaveKal Research

the U.S. net foreign debt today is much less than the accumulated current account deficits of the past 20 years.

Figure 2.2 shows the comparison between the U.S. net foreign debt and net foreign investment income.

Figure 2.2 shows that the United States presently has a net foreign debt of $2.5 trillion, and it also shows that the United States earns about $30 billion from these foreign negative assets. In other words, the United States is earning net money on its foreign debt. With a positive cash flow from its indebtedness, the argument that the U.S. foreign debt is unsustainable seems weak. If the United States is making money on its debt, it seems that the debt *is* sustainable.

This is not to say that large foreign debt and trade balance deficits are good things. The point is that economic principles from the past may not be as relevant today. We are seeking answers to the question of whether it makes sense to invest in stock markets today. And if so, what are the best investments to make?

We heard that there is a growing inordinate risk in the market, and we want to know if there is profit potential. At all times we must be cautious when we invest. But we must also guard against missing opportunities because things are not clear, or cannot be explained with formulas from the past.

Also important is the fact that people in emerging markets are accumulating wealth in places where there are weak property rights and political instability. If money from China or Saudi Arabia is invested in land and buildings in the United States, it benefits us all. The world is more interconnected, and the fruits of labor are invested where they might have a safe and continuous return. This also is a result of increased and more efficient globalization. The flow of money from these places to the United States, United Kingdom, Europe, and other Western countries, where property rights and the rule of law are strong, is expected to continue.

CONTINUED GLOBAL EXPANSION

As GaveKal and some other economists assert, there are reasons to believe that the global economy is far from collapsing. There are problems in the world, but there are still good reasons to be optimistic about the future and reasons to invest in the global markets.

Often things reported in the newspapers or on television are not as they seem. We hear reports about the U.S. negative balance of trade, low savings rate, and how manufacturing jobs are being shipped out of the United States. We hear that there is a race to the bottom in manufacturing costs, and that the middle class of America is being decimated. The fear is that this will spread to the middle classes around the world.

THE SHRINKING MIDDLE CLASS

Reports are common that jobs are diminishing for the middle class, and good jobs have been replaced by lower-paying jobs. The new jobs are accompanied by cutbacks in pension and health-care benefits. It is reported that the U.S. middle class is disappearing and being replaced by people working in menial jobs for low pay. There is some truth in this. But the conventional knowledge about a drop or even drift toward lower-paying jobs for a vast middle class is not the complete story, at least not according to Stephen Rose, author of *Social Stratification in the United States* (New Press, 2007). Rose makes the point that living standards for most Americans are improving, and that the middle class is shrinking because people are moving up on the income ladder, not falling down.

It is often stated that the U.S. median household income is $44,500. When the data forming this opinion is adjusted for such things as household size, and does not include those households headed by people younger than 29 or older than 59 (the beginning and end of people's working years when their earnings are lower), the typical American family median income jumps to $63,000. This is a fairly comfortable income for a middle-class family. It is not enough for an extravagant lifestyle, but is a livable amount.

It *is* true that the middle class is shrinking. From 1979 to 2004, Rose calculates that middle-class households—those with incomes of $30,000 to $75,000—declined about 13 percent. But the offset to this is that

Figure 2.3

Shrinking Middle-Class and Growing Affluence

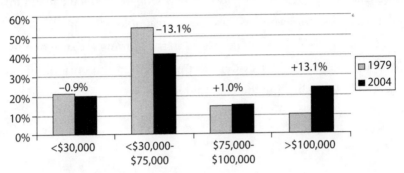

Source: Third Wave: A Strategy Center for Progressives

those households with incomes over $100,000 *rose* by about 13 percent. During this same time, the percentage of poor and near-poor households of less than $30,000 stayed about the same. The percentages of $75,000 to $100,000 also stayed about the same. See Figure 2.3.

Rose found that for married couples in all but the poorest households, income adjusted for inflation was higher in 2004 than in 1979, even after factoring in increases in spousal work hours. The fact that the American economy is producing low-paying jobs is not new. The number of lower-skilled jobs has been declining since 1979, but the number of elite high-paying jobs has been growing for years.

Mark A. Thoma, a professor in the Department of Economics, University of Oregon, sees reason to be optimistic about people in the American workforce. In his writings he notes that over 50 percent of Americans have no credit cards, and that only 1.5 percent of households declare bankruptcy in any given year. Professor Thoma calculates that middle-class assets have risen about 35 percent over the last 15 years. He also concludes that the percentage of companies offering retirement benefits has stayed about the same, and that the real shift has been from defined benefit plans to defined contribution. Insurance costs have risen, and employers and employees are paying more, but the premium share paid by employers has remained constant for 20 years.

The United States is a major player in the growing global economy, and this fact and other evidence conclude that the current global economy is not hurting the U.S. middle class.

Chapter | 3

POWERSHARES

PowerShares Capital Management, LLC, is an asset management firm headquartered in Wheaton, Illinois. The firm dedicates itself to creating intelligent ETFs and to this end uses sound portfolio construction and empirically verifiable investment management approaches. The firm offers ETFs in three ways.

The first is using intelligent indexing methodology that has been developed over a period of time. From this, ETFs are created that people can trade and invest in.

The second is to offer intelligent exposure, an example of which is the intelligent indexes created by Research Affiliates, a firm headed by Rob Arnott. PowerShares created fundamentally weighted ETFs that seek to replicate the performance, before fees and expenses, from indexes created by Research Affiliates.

Third, PowerShares is creating intelligent access, using intelligent methodologies developed by index creators, and packaging ETFs to replicate the performance of these indexes.

PowerShares offers these alpha-seeking ETFs to aid those searching to improve returns and lower risk.

USING INTELLIGENT ETFs

I remember when I learned about these unique offerings. Managing accounts and advising clients as a registered investment advisor, I was frustrated with the limited indexing possibilities with the then available ETFs.

While researching in June 2003, I noticed PWO and PWC, the first PowerShares ETFs. I was intrigued, but hesitated to buy because these ETFs were new, they had a small amount of shares outstanding, and trading in them was fairly light.

They kept performing well, and one thing comforted me about buying them: PWO and PWC ETFs, like most ETFs in this book, when they are created they buy the actual stocks making up the indexes they replicate. Because of this, market makers and specialists on the exchanges and traders on the Street are going to keep close any difference in the ETF value and its market price. Market prices usually stay close to the ETF net asset value because if they don't, market participants will arbitrage the differences, narrowing the spreads. The creation–redemption process pretty much ensures that buying or selling panics or any other pressures to force any over- or undersupply of tradable shares will rarely or never occur. This is a big difference between trading stocks and trading ETFs.

So I bought PWO and PWC and continued to study the intelligent, fundamentally weighted, magnified, and other unique ETFs.

From my experience managing accounts and advising people, I can attest to the effectiveness of the alpha-seeking new generation of ETFs. This is in addition to the usefulness of the original generation of ETFs. The revolution that has been spawned can be used to increase return. A lot of work from many people went into developing the original

ETFs. Back-testing and creating the new generation also has taken a lot of work, and traders and investors can profit from the new additions.

THE INTELLIDEX INDEX

PowerShares used the Intellidex Index to attempt to replicate their first ETFs, and this method has been expanded to some of their other ETFs. The first PowerShares ETF traded using the Intellidex Index methodology was PWC, which seeks to replicate a broad market segment.

ETFs based on the Intellidex Index are unique. The index has two primary objectives: The first is to control risk, and the second is to outperform, using its objective stock selection approach.

The ETFs constructed by PowerShares are not passive. Power-Shares thinks that one of the biggest misconceptions is that passive benchmarks fulfill the need of passive investors. If an investor believes that the market is efficient, or fairly so, a lot of investment literature advises that a benchmark is the best way to invest if one wants to follow a passive goal.

PowerShares has concerns with that view and thinks that imbedded in passive indexes are stock-specific risks that investors may not be aware of. In a broad market index, for instance, investors might assume that included in that group of stocks is a basket of small-, medium-, and big-cap companies. Often this is not the case. More likely, a few huge companies account for a large percentage of the big-cap ETFs, and secondarily a scattering of smaller companies.

Also what has to be considered is the performance of the industry sectors that go into making up the overall stock market.

Figure 3.1

The Different Asset Classes and How They Performed from 2001–2005

	Dynamic Industry Intellidex					S&P Super Composite Industry Index				
	2001	2002	2003	2004	2005	2001	2002	2003	2004	2005
	28.84%	−2.87%	99.74%	47.22%	62.30%	18.58%	1.40%	90.35%	35.96%	61.93%
	22.18%	−3.53%	66.37%	38.67%	55.04%	1.78%	−3.20%	77.79%	34.93%	49.67%
	19.06%	−5.77%	56.89%	30.40%	18.96%	−1.02%	−7.17%	54.99%	34.77%	33.31%
	9.46%	−6.93%	50.63%	26.04%	15.60%	−2.24%	−7.80%	46.16%	23.13%	16.88%
	4.27%	−7.74%	47.84%	22.49%	14.24%	−8.56%	−12.97%	42.93%	21.59%	15.21%
	0.94%	−8.10%	47.01%	21.62%	13.79%	−11.04%	−19.18%	35.26%	20.03%	14.75%
	0.14%	−8.82%	46.33%	20.47%	12.44%	−12.24%	−19.88%	30.77%	20.00%	14.00%
	−1.68%	−8.85%	45.81%	19.51%	12.22%	−12.71%	−22.50%	26.97%	15.99%	9.90%
	−4.59%	−10.64%	45.13%	19.01%	10.89%	−12.90%	−26.13%	26.68%	11.44%	2.73%
	−5.50%	−14.63%	38.68%	14.24%	6.77%	−15.62%	−28.00%	26.35%	9.06%	2.20%
	−9.04%	−18.06%	37.27%	11.04%	5.99%	−16.21%	−28.60%	24.47%	8.72%	1.29%
	−10.05%	−25.54%	36.83%	8.75%	5.30%	−16.71%	−29.10%	22.17%	8.28%	0.00%
	−12.82%	−35.95%	35.26%	8.46%	2.32%	−17.52%	−29.41%	21.13%	8.26%	−0.69%
	−22.39%	−38.54%	24.97%	2.25%	0.21%	−26.83%	−34.35%	18.92%	2.57%	−2.98%
	−22.66%	−43.05%	24.92%	−4.61%	−1.35%	−31.79%	−41.69%	18.49%	−2.38%	−5.71%
	−23.00%	−43.65%	15.94%	−5.97%	−6.76%	−33.09%	−42.94%	10.30%	−7.09%	−5.96%
	−41.36%	−45.23%	15.62%	−25.18%	−8.44%	−56.97%	−49.77%	7.31%	−21.42%	−12.89%
Yearly Return	−4.01%	−19.29%	43.25%	14.97%	12.91%	−15.01%	−23.61%	34.18%	13.17%	11.39%

Source: PowerShares Capital Management

Each year sectors perform differently. Not only is it sensible to diversify among different sectors for risk aversion, but for profit potential as well. Investors and traders must answer the question: what are the most promising sectors in which to trade and invest?

Along with sector choices is the decision to invest in a sector through an index that is primarily cap-weighted, or to invest through the new intelligent indexes, which are usually not strictly cap-weighted.

The results between these two indexes are shown in Figure 3.1. The sectors used in this figure are: Biotech, Food & Beverage, Leisure & Entertainment, Media, Networking, Pharmaceuticals, Semiconductors, Software, Building, Energy, Insurance, Oil & Gas Services, Retail, Utilities, Aerospace, Hardware, and Telecommunications. The sector index on the left is constructed in the Dynamic Industry Intellidex Index method, which is an intelligent index. The sector on the right, the S&P Super Composite Industry Index, is constructed in a more cap-weighted method.

In the years covered in Figure 3.1, the intelligent index outperformed. Also cap sizes can make a big difference in investment returns. Sometimes the preponderance of a few huge companies may not matter, and in fact may help performance. At other times this mix hinder performance. For instance, from 1995 to 2000 the big-cap indexes performed very well, so well that big-cap active money managers had a hard time keeping up with their performances.

What holders of ETFs that were attempting to replicate big-cap indexes may not have appreciated was that as the market kept gaining, the indexes were systematically gaining more exposure to the bigger, highest-capitalized companies. Companies such as Microsoft, Cisco, Intel, and other large-size tech companies were heavily weighted in these indexes.

From March 2000 to early 2007 the price performance would have a different scenario. The stocks that were leading the advance in 2000, many of them big-cap companies, have not advanced as much as have small- and mid-cap stocks. Many of the small- and mid-cap indexes have made new highs since 2000. Many big-cap general market indexes have not approached their highs of 2000. Clearly there was a risk in being in a concentration of big-cap stocks, and this risk continues. It is this risk that PowerShares and other alpha-seeking ETF providers are seeking to address.

Let's look at Figure 3.2 (on page 64), which shows the stock universe that the Intellidex Index considers.

The stock universe PowerShares considers is gleaned from very comprehensive company data encompassing 16,000 product levels. The data searches through product groups, subsectors, sectors, and

Figure 3.2

The Universe of PowerShares Investments, the Investable Portion They Use

The investable portion of the U.S. equity marketplace is defined to include U.S. domiciled companies on the three major exchanges. The Market Intellidex universe is defined as the 2,000 largest, most liquid stocks. The broad universe is divided into industry categories based on the Revere bottom-up approach and an Amex screening process, and then further by capitalization bands based on a fixed number of securities.

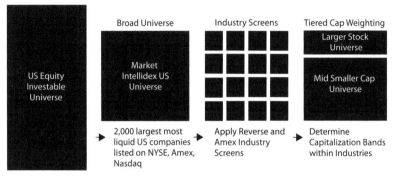

Source: PowerShares Capital Management

industries. Details of how the Intellidex makes its stock selection are not shared by the Intellidex architects.

SECTOR CONSIDERATION

This big-cap risk is magnified significantly when concentration is limited to only one or several sectors. In the sector cap-weighted ETFs, often the biggest cap-weighted companies make up the largest share of the index. Instead of getting equal exposure to, say, 70 companies, which would give broad sector exposure, in reality it might be that exposure is heavily weighted into about 10 companies or so. There is a possible built-in risk that you must be aware of. If the sector implodes, and big-cap stocks are the heaviest hit in that sector, this could cause a bigger loss than you thought you could have. In this case, the risk you were taking was bigger than you had envisioned.

It is not necessarily bad to have sector exposure to a handful of big-cap stocks that dominate an index. Having sector representation with a concentration of big-cap stocks could work in your favor. For instance, in the period of July 2006 to May 2007, the Select Sector Energy SPDR ETF (symbol XLE) advanced over 20 percent, which was a very good performance, outpacing the Dow Jones Industrial Average and many general market ETFs and sector ETFs. XLE's largest holding was ExxonMobil Corp. (symbol XOM). XOM comprised over 21 percent of the index.

This was a very good time to be in XOM and energy, and the position worked out very well. But there could be risk to this position, as evidenced by the technology sector implosion of the 2000 to 2003 period.

If you buy a cap-weighted ETF, you have to pay attention to the events in the five to ten companies that comprise the major weighting in the index. Much of that sector's ETF performance will be related to the performance of those big companies.

This does not lessen the fact that index investing through ETFs, even through cap-weighted ETFs, offers advantages over other ways of investing. Among its advantages is that ETFs are transparent, meaning you can easily see their holdings.

The concern is that buyers may get a false sense of diversification. Intellidex Indexes seek to control this diversification risk, and they do this through their portfolio-weighting approach. The index groups the stocks it is considering for index inclusion by category, and then into cap-size groups, and then stocks in each size group are weighted. The goal through building portfolios in this way is to achieve performance without stock-specific risk. To gain the right mix of market exposure, all Intellidex Indexes employ this weighted approach.

THE INTELLIDEX APPROACH AND ATTRIBUTION

Anytime an index deviates from a cap-weighted or float-weighted structure, there is attribution. A method for determining the reason for attribution consists of taking apart an index to study how its results were achieved, to understand where one index's performance came from compared to other indexes. The goal is to understand which factors made it possible for an index to add value. Included in the factors is to see if short-term trading added value, or if market timing added value, or if security selection added value. At times there will be attribution in ETFs, including PowerShares. For example, see Figure 3.3. The performance figures are hypothetical and do not reflect real performance.

The PowerShares Dynamic Software Intellidex Index often outperformed the conventional benchmark, which is the S&P Super Composite Software and Services Index. The S&P Software Index is a cap-weighted index. The PowerShares ETF that attempts to replicate the performance, not counting fees and expenses, of the Dynamic Software Intellidex Index trades under the symbol PSJ.

To see why an ETF is outperforming its benchmarks, you can look at the stocks that make up its benchmarks and analyze how they are faring. For the software sector relating to PSJ you could see how Microsoft or Adobe Systems is performing, two companies that usually have a heavy weighting in this sector. If Microsoft is up big, this could cause attribution, benefiting a cap-weighted ETF. If Microsoft is down big, intelligent ETFs such as PSJ will probably outperform the cap-weighted ETF.

The weighting approach used by the Intellidex Indexes was designed to control cap-size construction as a means to lower risk, not to create

Figure 3.3[1]

Dynamic Software Intellidex from PowerShares, SPY, and S&P Super Composite Software

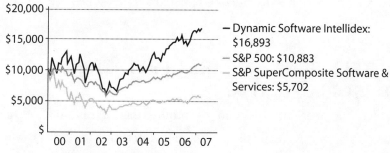

Source: PowerShares Capital Management

enhanced performances versus other indexes. The Intelligent Index cap-size construction method will create attribution, since there will be differences between PowerShares and other index constructions.

---

[1] The PowerShares Dynamic Software Portfolio (Fund) seeks to replicate, before fees and expenses, the Dynamic Software Index, which is designed to provide capital appreciation by thoroughly evaluating companies based on a variety of investment merit criteria, including fundamental growth, stock valuation, investment timeliness and risk factors.

Total Returns are based on the Closing Market Price. Performance data quoted represents past performance, which is not a guarantee of future results. Investment returns and principal value will fluctuate, and shares, when redeemed, may be worth more or less than their original cost. Current performance may be higher or lower than performance data quoted. After-tax returns reflect the highest federal income tax rate but exclude state and local taxes. Fund performance reflects fee waivers, absent which, performance data quoted would have been lower.

The Dynamic Software Intellidex Index return does not represent the Fund return. The performance results shown are hypothetical and reflect the investment returns that might have been achieved by investing $10,000 according to the Index on January 1, 2000. The results assume that no cash was added to or assets withdrawn from the hypothetical investment and that all dividends, gains, and other earnings in the account were reinvested in accordance with the Index's rules.

The Dynamic Software Intellidex does not charge management fees or brokerage expenses, and no such fees or expenses were deducted from the hypothetical performance shown. The Index does not lend securities, and no revenues from securities lending were added to the performance shown. You cannot invest directly in the Index. In addition, the results actual investors might have achieved would have differed from those shown because of differences in the timing, amounts of their investments, and fees and expenses associated with an investment in the Fund.

The Intellidex indexing method attempts to construct ETFs that provide diversification using its developed methodology, whether that helps or hurts its performances compared to other ETFs.

INTELLIGENT INDEXES IN RELATION TO STOCK PICKING

Often on television, the radio, or in other media, a pundit will say something like, "I really like companies with strong revenue growth, high expected sales growth, strong profit margins, and whose stocks have been laggards and are now starting to outperform." Or a money manager or analyst will opine on what moves stocks and give the above reasons or similar ones for buying a certain stock or basket of stocks.

Perhaps a market professional has found a system that works for her, but evidence shows that stock selection by money managers often does not beat the indexes over a period of time, especially in the bigger cap sizes. Money managers can have a niche, a way of investing, or a style that works for a time or in certain markets. Today's investors and traders have access to new methods to gain alpha and minimize risk. The bottom line for investors and traders is to make money, and knowing the truths that have been developed over a period of time can help make this possible.

Some aspects of the stock selection model used on Wall Street fly in the face of how empirical evidence is developed and used in other fields, such as medicine. When a person goes to a doctor, for instance, and that doctor prescribes medicine, the patient presumes the medicine prescribed has been tested. Patients assume there have been studies, both in laboratories and on test subjects, that have developed empirical evidence proving that the medicine is helpful, and in what ways. The assumption by patients is that all medicines are developed this way.

The prevailing mechanism of Wall Street stock selection is not established in this way. Not that Wall Street has to follow a pharmaceutical model, but some exploration of ways to gain alpha and to determine if a method works, and to what degree, seems the minimum that should be explored, considering all the money involved in the financial world.

Factors such as strong revenue growth, high expected sales growth, strong profit margins, and other items that are suggested by experts and pundits can make stocks go higher. However, it is rare to see it explained anywhere how these factors work together to affect stock prices. Studies have shown that there is very little correlation between the mentioned yardsticks and future market performance. In fact, some of the factors given as positive stock assumptions in reality have strong negative correlations to future performance. See Figure 3.4.

Sometimes sales growth might impact a stock's market price, but as Figure 3.4 shows, studies show that this factor alone may not mean a stock will go higher. In fact, this study shows that chasing sales growth can be counterproductive. The concern is that analysts, talking heads on television, and other experts might pore over income statements, balance sheets, and other company documents looking for reasons to buy stocks, and come to reasonable assumptions that a basis exists to buy a stock. But the risk in this method is that these assumptions could be wrong. In fact, empirical evidence suggests that analysts do not have all the answers to making money in the stock market. Let's look at Figure 3.5.

Figure 3.4

Does Strong Sales Growth Lead to Future Gains? Not Necessarily.

You may hear an analyst or money manager mention the fact that a company has strong sales growth, or ``top-end'' growth. Although this may sound exciting, an empirical analysis of sales suggests that perhaps it's detrimental to chase companies exhibitingthe strongest sales growth.

Two-Year Sales Growth Cross-Sectional Performance Average 6-Month Performance from '83 - '02 2,000 Largest U.S. Companies

As measured by the Information Coefficient (IC), sales growth is slightly negatively correlated to future performance, and companies experiencing the strongest sales growth are not the strongest performers.

Highest Sales Growth
IC = -0.008

Lowest Sales Growth
Each bar represents 200 stocks

Source: PowerShares Capital Management

Figure 3.5

Sell-Side Analyst Consensus Rating and What that Means

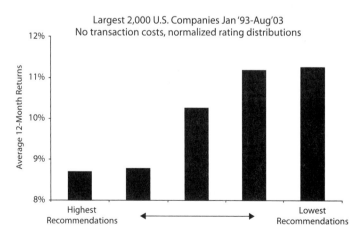

Largest 2,000 U.S. Companies Jan '93-Aug '03
No transaction costs, normalized rating distributions

Highest Recommendations

Lowest Recommendations

Source: PowerShares Capital Management

Figure 3.5 shows that the analysts' highest recommended stocks underperformed the analysts' lowest recommended stocks. Part of the reason may be that some analysts may not fully appreciate which factors have the most bearing on what moves stocks. Analysts are usually highly trained and competent but in this sampling the stocks they have highly recommended have underperformed.

Compared to work done by analysts, the Intellidex Index attempts to bring an objective management approach to the evaluation of stocks, and the index's goal is to find the right stocks to place in the index. The Intellidex method follows an empirical approach to index structuring. Its underlying philosophy is to search for stocks with the greatest consensus error, and uncover stock situations where the consensus outlook is most inaccurate.

In the traditional research process, analysts study companies and, after assessing their financial reports and forecasts, they estimate future earnings. They then render an opinion to buy or sell the stock or advise others to take this action.

With empirical research the premise is that stocks will move in the same direction as investors' expectations change, and that stocks will adjust accordingly. The goal is to look for the most mispriced stocks, not necessarily the best companies. The most mispriced stocks as priced in the markets, as seen by Intellidex, will be placed into the index.

DEVELOPMENT OF THE INTELLIDEX INDEX

The index is developed in a two-stage process. The first stage is a univariate research step, and the second step is a multivariate research step.

Univariate research evaluates individual company factors, such as price to book, price to sales, changes in consensus analysts' opinions, earnings revisions, and short-interest changes. More than three hundred factors are considered in constructing the index. These factors are then tested according to the model's methods.

The Intellidex Index method of modeling is not like other processes. For instance, it is not like the "Dogs of the Dow" method, in which the highest-yielding 10 stocks from the Dow Jones Industrial Average are selected and performance is tracked. Consistently these 10 stocks have outperformed the Average. In the Dow Dog method only 30 stocks are sampled, which is a very small universe. Because there are so few stocks in this method, there is often a one-stock surprise that can magnify performance.

For instance, inclusion of Altria Corp. (MO) in the Dow Dog group over the last two years, when this stock has climbed sharply, has helped performance. The back-tested performance numbers look better than they would have without this holding. One stock can make a large difference, which is a narrow view when making a long-term investment decision.

The Intellidex Index, by comparison, measures individual factors through broad sample sizes. For example, when studying dividend yield stocks, the Intellidex Index weighs how dividend yields are effective on a broad sample size of dividend-paying companies. The index measures the correlation of the yield to the future performance of the company's stock in the marketplace. Intellidex gathers data on the highest-yielding companies and compares this group to the lowest-yielding companies. Research shows that the higher-yielding companies do tend to outperform the lower-yielding companies in the stock universe.

Most important in this research is the Information Coefficient (IC). For instance, say that in its research the Intellidex Index assigns an IC to a company of .057. That number means that the dividend yield explains about 5.7 percent of future performance. That number is based on normalized data, not on raw data or actual returns. Normalized data is compiled by taking information that has been distilled from actual performance to ranked performance, and actual yield to ranked yield, and then comparing the two sets of information.

FALSE SIGNALS AND INTUITIVE STOCK SELECTION

This method removes false signals associated with much data used in back-testing. This can be examined by reviewing Figure 3.4, which shows that strong sales do not necessarily lead to higher stock prices. As pointed out in that figure, many analysts point to the higher sales factor as an important one. Intuitively, the idea that high sales growth leads to a higher stock price makes sense, and also the theory that companies that rapidly increase their revenues should be exciting to market investors and traders. However, when analyzed empirically, we see that this is not the case.

Figure 3.5 shows that in reality companies with the highest sales growth tend to underperform companies with the middle sales growth; companies with low sales growth or negative sales growth tend to underperform. One explanation could be that a company with strong revenue growth is obviously a very good company, but the market has probably already priced this growth into the stock price. This is the theory and type of company the Intellidex Index does not want to chase.

This empirical research was done in individual factors to determine whether these factors were predictive and useful for inclusion in the Intellidex model. After studying individual factors, the next step is to determine how the factors interact with each other and which factors should be brought into the model.

FACTORS INCLUDED IN THE INTELLIDEX MODEL

PowerShares believes there is a limit to the factors that can be correlated to predict future performance. Independent, different bits of information have to be used in model building, and correlation to each other of all individual factors in a model have to be independent of each other.

A sports analogy may be helpful. Suppose that instead of picking stocks, the model is used to assemble a winning basketball team. Theoretically, the model would note that height is correlated with exceptional basketball players, and that a player's weight has a correlation to outstanding performance. So height and weight are correlated to each other as characteristics of good players. Therefore, the model has to determine how these factors should be used together and how they work independently. The model could be structured to help build a basketball team or the principles adjusted for a stock selection model.

THE INTELLIDEX INDEX STOCK-PICKING MODEL

In evaluating stocks the Intellidex stock-picking model employs 25 independent factors. These factors are characterized into four perspectives to increase clarity. The index uses seven fundamental growth factors, which account for 28 percent of the model; seven valuation factors, which account for 29 percent of the model; six timeliness factors, accounting for 28 percent; and five risk factors, which account for 15 percent of the model. These factors are shown in Figure 3.6.

Intellidex does not disclose the factors used in its modeling. However, disclosure of some insights into each of the categories used is given. Some of the factors used in weighing the fundamental growth items are accounts receivable, asset turnover, inventory accrual, changes

Figure 3.6

The Intellidex Stock Evaluation Process—the Different Perspectives

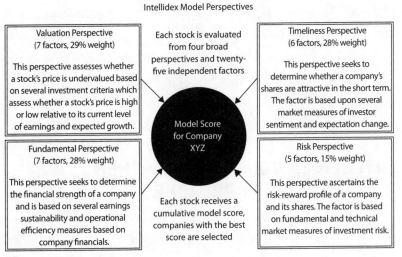

Intellidex Model Perspectives

Valuation Perspective (7 factors, 29% weight)	Each stock is evaluated from four broad perspectives and twenty-five independent factors	Timeliness Perspective (6 factors, 28% weight)

This perspective assesses whether a stock's price is undervalued based on several investment criteria which assess whether a stock's price is high or low relative to its current level of earnings and expected growth.

Model Score for Company XYZ

This perspective seeks to determine whether a company's shares are attractive in the short term. The factor is based upon several market measures of investor sentiment and expectation change.

Fundamental Perspective (7 factors, 28% weight)

Risk Perspective (5 factors, 15% weight)

This perspective seeks to determine the financial strength of a company and is based on several earnings sustainability and operational efficiency measures based on company financials.

Each stock receives a cumulative model score, companies with the best score are selected

This perspective ascertains the risk-reward profile of a company and its shares. The factor is based on fundamental and technical market measures of investment risk.

Source: PowerShares Capital Management

in volume in the company's stock, price to cash flow from operations, and the persistence of earnings surprises.

Some of the valuation factors used are price to cash flow, changes in debt relative to assets, comparison of actual to estimated earnings, earnings yields based on earnings estimates, price to operating income, changes in number of shares outstanding, and the amount of short interest.

Momentum factors used include short-term changes in free cash flow; earnings revisions, including present fiscal year and the future fiscal year; price changes of the stock; price changes relative to the stock's sector; changes in analysts' sentiment; and short interest change.

Risk factors examine the coefficient of variation of earnings, which weighs current earnings relative to historical earnings, analyzing the existence and amount of variability in earnings, and evaluating earnings sustainability. Also, this factor looks at the sustainability of the current forecast as compared to the company's long-term earnings forecast by analysts. This factor also analyzes the coefficient of variation of sales, and earnings growth rate.

These factors are some of the considerations incorporated into the Intellidex model, and are used to weight and select stocks to put into the index.

INTELLIDEX COMPARED TO OTHER QUANTITATIVE APPROACHES

The Intellidex Index employs what it calls a "sum of the evidence" approach, a multifactor model using 25 factors to evaluate securities. This method compares favorably to sequential screening models, which analyze companies with, among other possible parameters, low price to earnings ratios. After these models sift through a universe of stocks, finding those that most closely fit their models and the models consider these the attractive companies to buy, they whittle this stock universe down even further. Then these models will bring in other measurements, such as strong revenue growth or strong price changes in the last six months or so. The screening model approach, since it has a limited stock universe, runs the risk of excluding important companies.

Returning to the basketball team analogy, consider that in picking players for a team, a method should not exclude a player because he or she does not meet a height requirement. If a male player is less than six feet five inches tall, for example, he would not be automatically excluded just for that reason. If six feet five inches, according to the model, is a positive height for the team, and he is shorter but he has real ability, obviously he could be included on the team. In the sequential screening approach, this player would be cut on the basis of height. This is a shortcoming in the screening model approach. PowerShares believes that the Intellidex Index method using the sum of the evidence approach is superior.

Another model commonly used is the *dividend discount* method, which is very sensitive to model data input. This method is contrasted with the Intellidex multifactor approach, which looks at many different factors. The dividend discount model, PowerShares believes, tends to deaden the information coming into the model by looking only at ranked performance and not actual performance, thereby normalizing the information.

There are also a number of simplistic methods available for measuring stocks and building models. Some systems make simplistic weighting by earnings or by revenues. Weighting portfolios on one factor such as dividend yield creates a problem in that the model does not have the sum of the evidence or a full picture of the company.

Another sports analogy may be useful. Instead of stock picking, one could be comparing recruiting coaches. One recruiting coach is looking at players based on many different facets regarding what the player can contribute. Another coach bases her opinion only on how tall the player is. The coach who is considering height only will end up with a tall team, but that is not necessarily enough to win.

The coach who has many variables to consider will undoubtedly come up with a better team, since his selection is based on many independent factors. As far as stock selection, the Intellidex approach, which is broad and multifactored, is thought by PowerShares to be a much more beneficial approach to stock selection than other approaches.

INTELLIDEX COMPARED TO FUNDAMENTALLY WEIGHTED INDEXES

Intellidex indexing is different from fundamentally weighted indexing. Fundamentally weighted indexing attempts to address the cap-weighting indexing problem of having market price dictate portfolio construction.

Fundamentally weighted portfolios do not select and remove securities based on investment merit. Rather, fundamental weighting creates exposure through the included companies' footprints in the economy rather than letting the stock market price of the companies dictate their degree of inclusion.

Distributions are different in fund weighting compared to cap weighting, therefore making it possible for fundamental portfolios to avoid getting caught up in irrational exuberance such as the market experienced with technologies in the late 1990s.

The Intellidex Index is constructed for different reasons than fundamentally weighted portfolios. It evaluates securities for their investment merit and excludes securities when they no longer fit. This is evident from the higher turnover in an Intellidex versus a fundamentally weighted portfolio.

INTELLIGENT ETFs EXPAND TO THE GLOBAL MARKETPLACE

PowerShares is continuing in the intelligent ETF revolution, offering more ways to participate in the growth of the global economy and markets. Among its offerings are ETFs offering participation in non-U.S. stocks. In June 2007 PowerShares offered three new non-U.S. intelligent ETFs and will offer more ways of participating in the global marketplace in the future. See Figure 3.7.

Figure 3.7[2]

QSG Performance, SPY, and MSCI EAFE Comparison

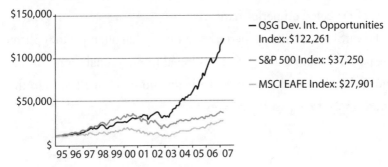

Source: PowerShares Capital Management

Figure 3.7 shows the hypothetical performance of the QSG Developed International Opportunities Index. The return does not represent the index return. The performance results shown reflect the investment returns that might have been achieved by the index. The index was constructed by a methodology developed by QSG Service Group.

---

[2] Total Returns are based on the Closing Market Price. Performance data quoted represents past performance, which is not a guarantee of future results. Investment returns and principal value will fluctuate, and shares, when redeemed, may be worth more or less than their original cost. Current performance may be higher or lower than performance data quoted. After-tax returns reflect the highest federal income tax rate but exclude state and local taxes. Fund performance reflects fee waivers, absent which, performance data quoted would have been lower.

The QSG Developed International Opportunities Index return does not represent the Fund return. The performance results shown are hypothetical and reflect the investment returns that might have been achieved by investing $10,000 according to the Index on January 1, 1995. The results assume that no cash was added to or assets withdrawn from the hypothetical investment and that all dividends, gains, and other earnings in the account were reinvested in accordance with the Index's rules.

The QSG Developed International Opportunities Index does not charge management fees or brokerage expenses, and no such fees or expenses were deducted from the hypothetical performance shown. The Index does not lend securities, and no revenues from securities lending were added to the performance shown. You cannot invest directly in the Index. In addition, the results actual investors might have achieved would have differed from those shown because of differences in the timing, amounts of their investments, and fees and expenses associated with an investment in the Fund.

QSG evaluates, ranks, and sorts more than 10,000 global securities using a proprietary multifactor model that is based on numerous measures of expected outperformance.

PowerShares has launched PFA, an ETF that attempts to replicate the performance of the QSG Developed International Opportunities Index, less fees and expenses. To learn more about PFA and other offerings, go to www.powershares.com.

Chapter | 4

WAYS TO WEIGHT INDEXES

The best-known index is the S&P 500, which was launched in 1957. At that time it was the first capitalization-weighted index. Capitalization (cap) weighting weights companies by the number of shares outstanding multiplied by the companies' market price. The bigger a company is, the higher percentage of that company's stock is represented in the index. Since the market cap is partly created by the price of the stock, the market essentially is valuing the company, which affects the index because of the weighting the company will be given.

The cap-weighted method is 50 years old and has been criticized since its inception. Most of the criticism centers on the fact that when a stock has a high price it might be overvalued, and when there are many shares outstanding, the market cap might be too high. This method could mistakenly overweight the overvalued companies and, conversely, with stocks that are too cheap, lead the index to underweight the undervalued companies.

If a stock is really in favor, with buyers driving up the price to, say, double what it previously was, the index might have to double its holding of that stock. And as traders know, at times they want to lighten up, not buy more of an up stock.

Cap-weighting indexers disagree. They say that unless one knows the true fair market value of a stock and unless it can be established which companies are overvalued and which undervalued, the perceived shortcomings of cap-weighted inefficiencies are interesting and maybe have some validity, but are basically useless.

RESEARCH AFFILIATES AND FUNDAMENTAL WEIGHTING

Rob Arnott argues that he has found a better way to weight indexes. As the head of Research Affiliates, based in Pasadena, California, he has constructed the FTSE RAFI US 1500 Small/Mid-cap index and the FTSE RAFI US 1000 index.

PowerShares has launched ETFs that seek to replicate, before fees and expenses, the performance of these indexes. They trade under the symbol PRFZ for the 1500 Small/Mid-Cap and PRF for the 1000 Index. The 1000 Index is designed to track the performance of the largest U.S. equities, which are selected on the basis of the following four fundamental measures of firm size: book value, cash flow, sales, and dividends. The 1,000 equities with the highest fundamental strengths are weighted by their fundamental scores. The fundamentally weighted portfolio is rebalanced and reconstituted annually.

The PowerShares FTSE RAFI US 1500 Small/Mid-Cap ETF tracks the performance of small and medium-sized U.S. companies. As mentioned above, companies are selected based on the following four fundamental measures of size: book value, cash flow, sales, and dividends. The fundamentally weighted portfolio is rebalanced and reconstituted annually.

Figure 4.1

A Spectrum of Returns: Where Were You Invested These Past Five Years?
Asset Classes and Five-Year Returns, 10-Year Characteristics

	Five-Year Returns		10-Year Characteristics	
Asset Class	**2001–2005**	**1996–2000**	**Std Dev**	**Correl w/60–40**
Emerging Market Stocks	143%	–18%	25%	68%
Commodities + TIPS	87%	55%	15%	9%
REITs	86%	46%	15%	29%
Emerging Market Bonds	79%	92%	16%	58%
S & P 500 Equal Weight	*51%*	*120%*	*18%*	*90%*
TIPS	51%	22%	6%	1%
High-Yield Bonds	46%	28%	7%	53%
Long-Term Govt Bonds	42%	42%	9%	1%
Lehman Aggregate	*33%*	*37%*	*4%*	*9%*
GNMA Bonds	29%	40%	3%	14%
Convertible Bonds	27%	75%	14%	76%
Unhedged Foreign Bonds	26%	–12%	8%	0%
Money Markets	12%	34%	1%	6%
S & P 500	*1%*	*132%*	*16%*	*99%*
Hedged EAFE	–1%	29%	15%	68%

It was only a bear market for those with an equity-centric portfolio.

Source: Research Affiliates

the bottom performers of the last five years—the S&P 500—and putting those funds into the best performer—emerging markets stocks.

The emerging market stocks' performance over the last five years is in the past. The past is not prologue, certainly not in the stock market.

Look at the prior five years in Figure 4.1—the years 1996–2000. If you were considering what asset class to invest in back in January 2001, you might have looked at Figure 4.1 and seen that emerging market stocks did not perform, that they were down 18 percent. Wanting to be more aggressive, you could have put your money into what was then performing—growth and technology—and bought the S&P 500, which was heavy in growth and technology and had returned 132 percent the prior five years.

In the next period the first performer dropped close to last place, and the bottom performer rose to first place. This happens more often than you would think in the stock market.

It is interesting to note the performance of the S&P 500 Equal Weight Index. The S&P 500 Equal Weight Index weights each company in its portfolio equally, meaning that each stock represents 0.2 percent of the portfolio. And, unlike a purely passive index, this index keeps the weighting at 0.2 percent, with rebalancing done quarterly by the selection committee. This is very different than a cap-weighted index.

Figure 4.1 shows that over the most recent five-year period the Equal Weight S&P 500 Index was up 51 percent. The S&P 500 Index was up only 1 percent. That is a large gap that is worth exploring.

At the start of the second five-year period, the S&P 500 was heavily weighted in some of the highest multiple companies in the history of U.S. capital markets. In January 1995, the index was invested in about 11 percent technology, and in March 2000 that sector had grown to have a 34 percent weighting. It was risky to have about a third of the index in technology. But the index is transparent, and investors and traders could easily see this sector weighting and they could avoid the index if they wished. Technology at that time, however, seemed invulnerable to reverses. The S&P 500 Index was heavily concentrated in stocks of the technology sector *because* of the stocks' high multiples. This is the nature of the cap-weighting system. Meanwhile, the average index stock was more moderately priced and the average stock performed adequately.

One of the surprises discovered by Rob Arnott in analyzing the market of the last five years is that the bull market of the 1990s did not end for most companies until April 2002. So the bull market of the 1990s continued for two years after the tech stock bubble burst. Finally, the average stocks joined in and the entire market entered a bear phase beginning in April 2002. That bear market ended six months later and recovered well, going to a new high in the third quarter of 2003. That is what the average stock did in the market, and the cap-weighted indexes produced poorer results than the average stock.

The market in the second five-year period (shown in Figure 4.1) rewarded value stocks and small-cap stocks. The S&P 500 Equal Weight Index has a value tilt, and value stocks drove its good returns.

In the previous five-year period, which was a period that favored growth stocks, the S&P 500 Index outperformed the S&P 500 Equal Weight Index. But the equal-weighted performance, even without the heavy tech concentration, was very good, returning 120 percent versus the S&P 500 return of 132 percent. The equal-weighted index gave up very little for not having a tech concentration.

THE PERFORMANCE-DRAG PROBLEM

What does one find when considering the 10 top companies by market capitalization? Generally, one finds companies that are huge, very respected, and expected to become even bigger over time. If we follow fundamental reasoning as espoused by Research Affiliates, if market price equals true, fair value, plus or minus a large error (the error being uncertainties relating to the unknowable future), then it would be expected that some companies would migrate to a higher market capitalization than they deserve. Those companies would be overvalued.

Consider the top 10 highest capitalized stocks today and imagine what might happen to those companies 20 years in the future. In 20 years investors would probably look back and see that some of the top 10 stocks were excellent and really did deserve a top 10 ranking.

But what about the other top 10 stocks? There is a good chance people will reflect, shake their heads, and wonder what the market was thinking, assigning a top 10 ranking to some companies that did not deserve that high a market-cap weighting. These companies, the ones with an undeserved multiple, will put a drag on index performance. Investors cannot know which companies these are, but these companies will definitely hurt the indexes they are in.

Research Affiliates has found that over the last 80 years, on a rolling 10-year basis, 3 out of 10 of the top 10 stocks on the market-cap rosters outperformed the average stock, and 7 out of 10 underperformed. That is not a good performance. An index that has wrong stocks 7 out of 10 times has a performance drag that can cost you money.

It is helpful to consider by what margin the top 10 stocks underperformed. Research Affiliates found that it was substantial. The underperforming stocks were down by an average of 26 to 30 percent. But these are only 10 stocks. Since this is so few, one wonders if it makes a real difference that they underperformed. The difference is very important, because these 10 stocks comprise about 25 percent of the indexes most of the time. If an index has a quarter of its money in stocks that underperform by 26 percent or more of their starting value, then that is an index that has a built-in structural drag on performance.

FIXING THE PERFORMANCE-DRAG PROBLEM

It is helpful to know more about the performance-drag problem to understand how it can be fixed.

According to Rob Arnott, cap weighting introduces a substantial growth bias into an index. Growth companies in the index usually have higher multiples, which means investors think future prospects for those companies are very attractive. The growth bias by itself does not hurt investors, the companies usually *do* have superior growth, and sometimes this growth is sufficient to justify their high multiple. That growth bias is not always a help because if the market is doing its job correctly, which is assessing companies and having them sell according to their true value in the market, those companies will be priced at just high enough multiples sufficient to offset their future growth. The future returns on those stocks for investors will then be the same as the future returns for the other stocks in the market.

But the market does not always keep multiples low enough for growth stocks. At certain times this growth bias helps an investor; at other times it does not help, and it may even hurt. This bias would have to be corrected for an investor to receive a return more truly tied to the overall market.

Unfortunately, as far as risk is concerned, Research Affiliates is of the opinion that cap-weighted indexes often ensure that investors have peak exposure to a stock, sector, or general market at a peak just before a bubble bursts. Consequently, investors wind up pursuing the latest fads, with high expectations, and they shun the stocks and assets that are most out of favor because of an inherent, structural result of the characteristics of the cap-weighting method. Studies show that the most important problem with cap weighting is that it tends to overweight every overvalued company and underweight every undervalued company. A possible way to correct this structural problem is to weight the index equally, and ignore market price, valuation multiples, and other similar factors. One way to do this is to use the size of the companies in the index calculations.

MEASURING COMPANY WORTH

A company size can be measured in many ways. It can be evaluated by amount of profits, sales totals, book value, dividends, or by all sorts of other ways. All of this affects an index's returns. Research has shown that if weighting is done on any of the measures or other evaluations mentioned here on a long-term basis, materially higher rates of return can be achieved.

This leads to the question of which measure or measures should be used to evaluate companies. In measuring companies for index uses, research done by Research Affiliates suggests that perhaps no one single measure leads to an ideal and complete picture of a company or group of companies. Just like a footprint in the sand has multiple measurements, such as length and width and depth, the footprint that a company has in the economy has different measurable aspects. Some sort of composite measure of the aggregate scale of a company's place in the economy can be determined by using its multiple measures.

For example, General Electric (symbol GE) is 4 percent of the U.S. economy as measured by dividends, 3 percent of the U.S. economy by sales and profits, and 2 percent by book value. There could be an argument about whether GE is 2, 3, or 4 percent of the economy, leading to an agreement that the numbers could be averaged. The agreement could be that GE is 3 percent of the economy, and that would be GE's representation in the index.

It does not matter what exact number is used, and the weighting does not have to be precisely right. The approximate weighting should go into the index portfolio, and the weight has to be independent from over- or undervaluation (caused by linking weighting to the price of the stock). In fundamental weighting, it is not wise to let the market determine the company weightings that go into an index.

By using the fundamental type of approach—selecting, ranking, and weighting companies by fundamental measures of scale of a company—the linkage between portfolio weight and over- and undervaluation is stripped away.

CREATING INDEX PORTFOLIOS OF UNIQUE CHARACTERISTICS

To see the difference in performance of different indexes, see Figure 4.2.

In Figure 4.2, the gray line shows the performance of a cap-weighted index containing the 1,000 largest companies, selected on the basis of and weighted by market cap. This is a typical method for constructing a cap-weighted index. It is similar to the stock construction of the Russell 1000 Index, and is also similar to the sector allocation weightings for the S&P 500 Index.

A dollar invested in this index in 1961, with the index rebalanced every year to the new 1,000 largest companies, would have paid off handsomely. At the end of 2005 each dollar put into the index would have grown to $73. Seventy-three times your money is a great result. But not as great as receiving 166 times your invested dollar.

Notice the black line in Figure 4.2. This line traces the performance of the stocks of the average company weighted by and selected by the fundamental size of those companies. This fundamentally weighted index would have returned $166 for every dollar invested. The index also would have performed well in the period when the bubble burst for technology stocks. When that bubble burst, the gray

Figure 4.2
_____

Comparison of Indexes. U.S. Fundamental Index (RAFI) 1000 vs.
Cap-Weighted U.S. 1000

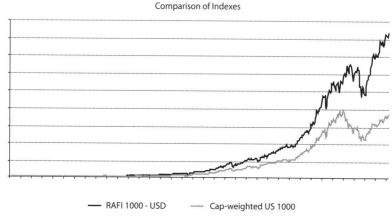

Source: Research Affiliates

line, which is the cap-weighted index performance, dove into a two-and-a-half-year bear market, taking down index valuations by almost half. The black line, mirroring the performance of the average company, consists of a different universe than the cap-weighted stocks. This line continued rising for two more years than the gray line, and the bull market of the 1990s for this index did not end until April 2002. The black line index had a short, sharp six-month bear market, recovered to new highs by the third quarter of 2003, and by late 2006 this index was about 60 percent above the levels at the bubble peak.

Studies done by Research Affiliates conclude that a fundamentally weighted index adds value just when the added-on value is needed the most. Historically, during bear markets, fundamentally weighted indexes have outperformed cap-weighted indexes by about 5 percent.

There is also comparative return between weighting methods. Research Affiliates concludes that in markets up around 20 to 30 percent a year for five years, sometimes fundamentally weighted indexes perform better than and sometimes not as well as cap-weighted indexes. Sometimes there is very little difference between the two. Markets that are up 20 to 30 percent a year for five years are major bull markets. In a moderate bull market, one with 10 to 20 percent annual returns, fundamentally weighted indexes usually win. In a disappointing market with 10 percent annual returns or lower, research shows that fundamental indexing almost always beats cap-weighted indexes, often by a large margin. This may be because there is a lot of rotation in the top companies in the cap-weighted indexes.

STOCK ROTATION IN DIFFERENT WEIGHTED INDEXES

To explore this, look at Figure 4.3. This figure looks back at the top 10 companies by S&P market capitalization, and divides the time segments into five-year segments since 1965.

In 1965 there were well-known companies such as AT&T, General Motors, Standard Oil of New Jersey (now part of Exxon Mobil Corp.), and other familiar names. Number six is Dupont. Dupont is no longer on the list five years later. It underperformed the average stock so badly that it tumbled from sixth place to off the list entirely. That disappointing performance affected the index negatively for the next five years.

Xerox replaces Dupont. Xerox was placed on the list in 1970 and was gone by 1975, never to return. Companies that disappeared from the list shortly after being added are "flip-flop" types. Flip-flops hurt the index twice: first because there were too few shares held when those companies soared in price, and once more because too many shares were held when their prices collapsed.

Listed are 23 "fallen angels," meaning that in the last 40 years, 23 of these companies have fallen from the list. There were 14 flip-flop companies in the last 40 years, each one hurting index performance twice.

Figure 4.3

Rotation in the Top 10 Cap-Weighted

	Cap Weighting, Top 10 Lists, January 1, 1965–2005									
Rank	1965	1970	1975	1980	1985	1990	1995	2000	2005	Summary Statistics
1	T	IBM	T	IBM	IBM	XON/XOM	GE	MSFT	GE	Fallen Angles
2	GM	T	IBM	T	XON/XOM	GE	T	GE	XOM	23
3	J/XOM	GM	XOM	XOM	GE	IBM	XOM	CSCO	C	Changes:
4	IBM	EK	EK	GM	GM	T	KO	WMT	MSFT	27/27
5	TX/CVX	J/XOM	GM	SN/AN	T	MO	MO	XOM	PFE	Flip/Flops:
6	DD	S	S	MOB/XOM	SUO	MRK	WMT	INTC	BAC	14
7	S	TX/CVX	PG	GE	SN/AN	BMY	MRK	LU	JNJ	Leads RAFI:
8	GE	XRX	GE	SD/CVX	DD	DD	IBM	IBM	IBM	23
9	GO/CVX	GE	SN/AN	ARC/AN	S	SN/AN	PG	C	AIG	Lags RAFI:
10	EK	GO/CVX	TX/CVX	SUO	EK	BLS	DD	AOL	INTC	36
Additions/ Subsequent Deletes		1/2	2/4	4/3	3/4	4/3	3/6	6/4	4	

Source: Research Affiliates

Now look at Figure 4.4, which shows the same type of information as found in Figure 4.3, but uses fundamental ranking for weighting companies in the index.

General Motors, Standard Oil of New Jersey, and AT&T are still at the top of the list. Dupont is still number six and was not on the

Figure 4.4

Rotation in the Top 10 RAFI-weighted

	Fundamental Indexing, Top 10 Lists, January 1, 1965–2005									
Rank	1965	1970	1975	1980	1985	1990	1995	2000	2005	Summary Statistics
1	GM	T	T	T	T	XON/XOM	XON/XOM	XOM	XOM	Fallen Angels
2	T	GM	GM	GM	XON/XOM	IBM	IBM	F	C	7
3	J/XOM	J/XOM	J/XOM	XON/XOM	IBM	GM	GM	GM	GM	Changes
4	F	F	IBM	IBM	GM	F	F	GM	WMT	15/13
5	TX/CVX	IBM	TX/CVX	MOB/XOM	MOB/XOM	T	GE	C	FNM	Flip/Flops:
6	DD	TX/CVX	F	F	TX/CVX	MOB/XOM	T	T	BAC	1
7	GE	GO/CVX	GO/CVX	TX/CVX	SN/AN	GE	MOB/Acq'd	MO	T	Leads Cap:
8	S	MOB/XOM	MOB/XOM	GE	CHV/CVX	DD	MO	FNM	CVX	36
9	IBM	GE	SD/CVX	GO/Acq'd	GE	CVX	DD	WCOM	GM	Lags Cap:
10	SD/CVX	S	S	SD/CVX	DD	SN/AN	CHV/CVX	IBM	AIG	23
Additions/ Subsequent Deletes		2/1	1/1	1/1	2/1	1/1	1/2	3/4	4	

Source: Research Affiliates

index five years later. This is because fundamentally the size of the company declined in the next five years, and as a company it no longer ranked among the 10 largest.

The fundamentally-weighted index shows only seven fallen angels compared to 23 in the cap-weighted index, over the last 40 years.

There is only one flip-flop company, and exposure to that company would have hurt performance twice: once with too few shares in the index and once with too many shares in the index. This one company compares with 14 flip-flops in the cap-weighted index. This suggests more stability regarding stock selection and retention in fundamental weighting compared to cap weighting.

FUNDAMENTAL AND CAPITALIZATION WEIGHTING IN SECTOR WEIGHTING

In cap-weighted sectors there are wide variations over time in the different sectors' sizes, magnifying the various sectors' importance in the index. See Figure 4.5.

Figure 4.5

Sector Weights over Time, Cap Weighted

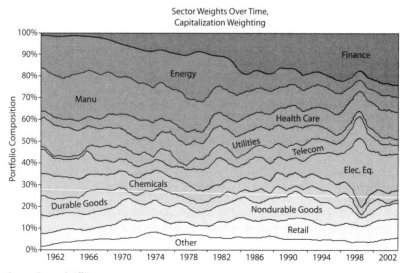

Source: Research Affiliates

To see how sector weightings changed, note the middle sector in Figure 4.5, which is identified by "Elec. Eq.," and is the electronic equipment sector. This sector represents the technology sector. This sector was big in the 1960s, small in the 1970s, big again in the 1980s, then it shrank before ballooning in the late 1990s, before shrinking again.

To see another example of sector weighting changes, look at the utilities band, located two bands above the technology band. The utility sector comprised 14 percent of the market total in the 1960s, and just 1 percent at the top of the technology bubble. Utilities, therefore, dropped from being more important than technology as a part of the market's assessment of the future economy in the 1960s and 1970s, to being insignificant when compared to the technology sector at the technology sector's peak. The market turned out to be wrong, since the utility sector has continued to be important to the economy.

When comparing cap-weighted and fundamentally weighted indexes, it appears that fundamentally weighted indexes did a better job of capturing the economy's evolution rather than chasing fads, bubbles, and shifting expectations. Now let's look at Figure 4.6.

The technology sector band was very steady in the 1960s, 1970s, and 1980s, and has been growing since that time. The economy is more technologically focused than in the past, and the index should have more technology sector representation, which it does. Utilities have dropped from 12 percent of the size of the market, fundamentally weighted, to 7 percent today, reflecting a steadily decreasing importance of this sector to the economy.

Research Affiliates has conducted analysis on all of the S&P sectors, and has concluded that 10 out of 10 sectors have had value added by fundamental weighting.

Discretionary spending stocks add about 1 percent per annum, on average, using fundamental weighting compared to cap weighting;

Figure 4.6

Sector Weights Over Time, Fundamentally Weighted

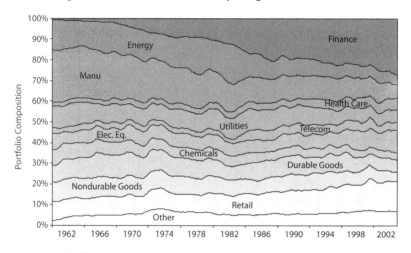

Source: Research Affiliates

consumer staples, energy, and financials, 3 to 4 percent value added per annum; health care, industrial, materials, 3 to 4 percent per annum; telecom, 2 to 3 percent added per annum; utilities, 7 percent per annum. These are very large gains and made just from weighting by fundamental factors, not from stock picking.

Fundamental weighting allows its index to keep pace with a sector, such as the information technology sector during a bubble, and during that sector's crash the impact should be softened. Fundamentally weighted indexes will suffer during market crashes, but are structured so that their suffering might be lessened; even subsequent recoveries to old highs are not impossible.

Figure 4.7 and Figure 4.8 illustrate the investment performance of some of the RAFI fundamentally weighted ETFs. To see the RAFI sector fundamentally weighted ETFs, other RAFI ETFs, and the full range of PowerShares ETFs, go to www.powershares.com.

Figure 4.7[1]

PowerShares FTSE RAFI U.S. 1500 Small-Mid Portfolio, FTSE RAFI vs. Russell 2000 vs. S&P Small Cap

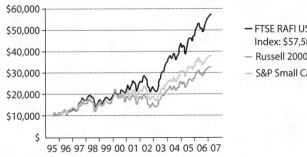

— FTSE RAFI US 1500 Small-Mid Index: $57,581
— Russell 2000 Index: $32,853
— S&P Small Cap Index: $38,347

Source: PowerShares Capital Management

[1] The PowerShares FTSE™ RAFI US 1500 Small-Mid Portfolio (Fund) seeks to replicate, before fees and expenses, the FTSE™ RAFI US 1500 Small-Mid Index. The objective of the Index is to track the performance of small and medium-sized U.S. companies. Companies are selected based on the following four fundamental measures of size: book value, cash flow, sales, and dividends. Each of the equities with a fundamental weight ranking of 1,001 to 2,500 is then selected and assigned a weight equal to its fundamental weight. The fundamentally weighted portfolio is rebalanced and reconstituted annually. Fund history and all inception performance are based on the Fund inception date: 9/20/2006.

All other index history is based on the available historical performance of the index.

Total Returns are based on the Closing Market Price. Performance data quoted represents past performance, which is not a guarantee of future results. Investment returns and principal value will fluctuate, and shares, when redeemed, may be worth more or less than their original cost. Current performance may be higher or lower than performance data quoted. After-tax returns reflect the highest federal income tax rate but exclude state and local taxes. Fund performance reflects fee waivers, absent which, performance data quoted would have been lower.

The FTSE˜ RAFI US 1500 Small-Mid Index return does not represent the Fund return. The performance results shown are hypothetical and reflect the investment returns that might have been achieved by investing $10,000 according to the Index on June 30, 1995. The results assume that no cash was added to or assets withdrawn from the hypothetical investment and that all dividends, gains, and other earnings in the account were reinvested in accordance with the Index's rules.

The FTSE˜ RAFI US 1500 Small-Mid Index does not charge management fees or brokerage expenses, and no such fees or expenses were deducted from the hypothetical performance shown. The Index does not lend securities, and no revenues from securities lending were added to the performance shown. You cannot invest directly in the Index. In addition, the results actual investors might have achieved would have differed from those shown because of differences in the timing, amounts of their investments, and fees and expenses associated with an investment in the Fund.

Figure 4.8²
_____

PowerShares FTSE RAFI US 100 Portfolio, FTSE RAFI vs. Russell 1000 vs. S&P 500

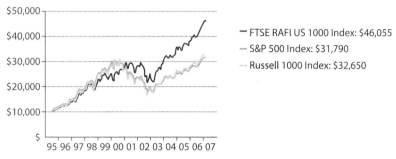

— FTSE RAFI US 1000 Index: $46,055
— S&P 500 Index: $31,790
— Russell 1000 Index: $32,650

Source: PowerShares Capital Management

_____

² Fund history and all inception performance are based on the Fund inception date: 12/19/2005. All other index history is based on the available historical performance of the index.

Total Returns are based on the Closing Market Price. Performance data quoted represents past performance, which is not a guarantee of future results. Investment returns and principal value will fluctuate, and shares, when redeemed, may be worth more or less than their original cost. Current performance may be higher or lower than performance data quoted. After-tax returns reflect the highest federal income tax rate but exclude state and local taxes. Fund performance reflects fee waivers, absent which, performance data quoted would have been lower.

The FTSE™ RAFI US 1000 Index return does not represent the Fund return. The performance results shown are hypothetical and reflect the investment returns that might have been achieved by investing $10,000 according to the Index on June 30, 1995. The results assume that no cash was added to or assets withdrawn from the hypothetical investment and that all dividends, gains, and other earnings in the account were reinvested in accordance with the Index's rules.

The FTSE⁻ RAFI US 1000 Index does not charge management fees or brokerage expenses, and no such fees or expenses were deducted from the hypothetical performance shown. The Index does not lend securities, and no revenues from securities lending were added to the performance shown. You cannot invest directly in the Index. In addition, the results actual investors might have achieved would have differed from those shown because of differences in the timing, amounts of their investments, and fees and expenses associated with an investment in the Fund.

Chapter | 5

RYDEX INVESTMENTS

Rydex Investments has been one of the leading investment firms in developing specialized and effective investments used in constructing and enhancing modern portfolios. Through its ongoing innovation, Rydex attempts to anticipate the evolving needs of investors. Rydex strives to serve investors and investment advisors, and encourages them to maximize the value of its investing tools and strategies.

Since its early days, when it launched its Rydex Nova Fund, the first leveraged mutual fund available to the public, Rydex has experienced impressive growth. Other industry innovations were the first short equity and fixed-income mutual funds, and an early security was the Rydex S&P 500 Equal Weight ETF (symbol RSP). Rydex manages more than $14 billion in assets, and offers over 80 mutual funds and ETFs.

THE RYDEX CURRENCYSHARES

Rydex offers a variety of securities called CurrencyShares. There are eight CurrencyShares available, all of which can be viewed on their CurrencyShares Web site, www.currencyshares.com.

CurrencyShares are structured differently than the usual equity ETFs. As differentiated from 1940-Act ETFs (which most equity ETFs are), CurrencyShares are 1933 Act securities. Generally, the 1933 Securities Act was enacted to give investors more information about the securities offered in the stock markets. The act legislated that there would be better disclosure by requiring companies to register with the Securities and Exchange Commission (SEC). Registration ensures that companies provide the SEC and potential investors with all relevant information. This information is in the prospectus and registration statement.

Most of the ETFs covered in this book are 1940 Act mutual funds. The 1940 Act set standards by which investment companies should be regulated. The act defined and regulated investment companies, including mutual funds.

The 1940 Act established that a Unit Investment Trust would be an investment company organized under a trust indenture, contract of custodianship agency, or a similar instrument. Other stipulations are that the investment company does not have a board of directors, that it issues redeemable securities, each of which represents an undivided interest in a unit of specified securities. This description does not include a voting trust.

Another type of investment company in the Act of 1940 is the Management Company. This includes any investment company other than a face-amount certificate company or a unit investment trust. The most well-known type of management company is the mutual fund.

The Rydex CurrencyShares are 1933 Act securities and are in essence guided by a grantor trust. Rydex and other ETF makers construct and distribute 1933 Act ETFs, and deal with advertising and other regulations according to SEC specifications. The 1933 Act ETFs could be using derivatives. A 1933 Act investment security is structured as a trust, and the trust doctrine explains to the holders of the trust what the trust can do. The trust is held to the mandate set forth in the trust, and cannot deviate from its mandate.

HOW RYDEX CURRENCYSHARES TRUSTS ARE STRUCTURED

Some trusts are dynamic in nature, especially those that replicate the price action of natural resources or commodities. Limited liability companies are usually set up to invest in the commodity, and then a trust is established to invest in the limited liability company (LLC). However, there are other ways to use trusts to invest in commodities or collectibles.

For example, the largest trust in the market is the State Street streetTRACKS Gold Shares Trust (symbol GLD), which trades as an ETF. GLD invests in gold bullion only. (There is actually a vault in London that houses $9 billion worth of gold for this trust.)

The streetTRACKS Gold Shares Trust is an investment trust that was formed on November 12, 2004, pursuant to a trust indenture. The trust holds gold, and from time to time, issues shares in exchange for deposits of gold and to distribute gold in connection with redemptions. The investment objective of the trust is for the shares to reflect the performance of the price of gold bullion, less the trust's expenses.

The Rydex CurrencyShares are structured in a similar fashion to GLD, as compared to other trusts that invest in limited liability companies. Currency trusts other than Rydex's ETFs are available in the market. Some of these are structured as grantor trusts, and instead of buying and holding the currency, as Rydex does, the ETFs invest in a limited liability company. The LLC invests in currency futures or other derivatives.

The GLD structure allows investors and traders to buy ETFs that are backed by the actual commodity or currency. The ETFs will fluctuate in price along with the currency or commodity price. They will also allow the holder to have direct participation rather than be affected by external pressures, such as derivative price movement or option supply and demand factors.

For example, if you wanted to buy Australian dollars, you can buy them cheaply, efficiently, and quickly through your brokerage account. You would simply buy FXA, which is the Rydex Australian dollar ETF.

Say that you are making a trip to Australia and are concerned that the Australian dollar will appreciate against your U.S. dollar, making your trip more expensive. Or maybe you just like Australia and think its dollar should be worth more versus the U.S. dollar and want to participate in its move. You would buy FXA in your brokerage account.

There are other ways you could participate in the move of the Australian dollar. You could use the futures market to buy the Australian dollar. You could go to a bank and exchange your dollars for Australian dollars.

You could also open an account at a broker or online broker such as Forex. One of the advantages of Forex and some other currency brokers is that you can use margin. These firms also specialize in trading in currencies, and offer investment advice and research.

ADVANTAGES OF THE RYDEX CURRENCYSHARES

Foreign currency investing has merit for investors and traders. They may be looking for diversification that is highly noncorrelated to stock market investments and noncorrelated to other asset classes, or want a hedge against a weakening U.S. dollar, or think the currency of a foreign country is undervalued.

People can buy and sell Rydex CurrencyShares through their brokerage accounts. There are advantages to buying currency this way. Like other ETFs you can buy FXA and other currencyshares on margin. In placing the order, you can use buy limits. While holding FXA, you can employ stop loss orders, and use any other order specifications generally used with securities.

If you do not like Australia and think that its dollar is going down, you can short FXA. Like other ETFs, you can short on a downtick. Shorting FXA is similar to going long the U.S. dollar versus the Australian dollar.

FXA only holds Australian dollars. Because of its trust mandate, this is all that it can hold. There is no advisor overseeing FXA and the other Rydex CurrencyShares. There is simply a sponsor and a trustee. Rydex is the ETF sponsor, and a bank is the trustee. A second bank is the depositor, which holds the Australian dollars for the trust. The trust process makes necessary a different creation and redemption process than the usual equity ETF process.

For the creation of new ETF shares, the market maker will deliver Australian dollars to the ETF creator. The ETF maker will deliver ETF shares. The ETF creator, in this case Rydex, will simply deliver the Australian dollars to the depositor bank. The bank will pay the Rydex Trust interest on the deposited Australian dollars. This interest accumulates in the Trust and is shared by the holders of the CurrencyShares.

OTHER RYDEX CURRENCYSHARES

The RydexCurrencyShares series is offered in eight different currencies. Among these are the British pound, Canadian dollar, and Euro

Trust. If you think, for instance, that the euro will appreciate in value, the Rydex CurrencyShares series is an efficient way to invest in the euro. You simply buy FXE, the euro currency ETF, and you own a portion of the shares that hold the euro in a bank.

There are often variances in the price of the trust and the value of its underlying currency. Often, a trust appears to be trading at a premium, especially near the end of the month. This is because of accrued interest that has accumulated in a trust. The ETF pays out the interest that it has earned on a monthly basis.

TAXES AND RYDEX CURRENCYSHARES

There is a tax disadvantage in holding certain assets, and this tax consequence relates even if the assets are held in 1933 Act ETFs, including the Rydex CurrencyShares series. For income tax purposes, the securities are deemed a "pass-through" for holding currencies. The IRS deems holding the Rydex CurrencyShares the same as holding currency. Therefore, there is no capital gains advantage, no matter how long you hold the currency or the Rydex CurrencyShares.

For example, if you buy foreign currency and sell it two years later at a profit, you are taxed at ordinary income rates. There is no long-term capital-gains tax advantaged rate. As far as the IRS is concerned, you were essentially holding the Australian dollar or euro or other currency. This is the same tax treatment as is given for many gold trust ETFs and other 1933 Act trust ETFs.

NONCORRELATION TO THE STOCK MARKETS

To hedge against holding a portfolio of U.S. stocks, buying currencyshares is a better hedge than buying foreign stocks. Foreign stock markets around the globe do have some correlation to the U.S. markets, with some markets more correlated than others. Foreign currencies have little or no correlation.

Instead of investing in one currency, some of the currency ETFs that invest in LLCs are structured to hold baskets of currencies. This contrasts with Rydex CurrencyShares, which hold a single currency, and hold the currency directly, with no derivatives (e.g., futures).

You may prefer to hold a basket of securities rather than a single country or region-specific currency. You may think that the U.S. dollar will underperform other currencies but are not sure which ones. In this case you may want to hold two or three currencies in your account. For diversification it may be better to spread the risk. This currency positioning is an efficient diversification strategy. For example, U.S. citizens probably have all their assets—house, car, stocks, and other assets—denominated in U.S. dollars. How can they diversify against a drop in the value of the dollar? Foreign stocks do not offer as effective a non-correlation investment against the dollar as foreign currencies do.

RYDEX ETFs

Rydex offers a full line of ETFs, including broad market, style, and sector ETFs. The Rydex ETFs are focused and structured around their overall strategies from an investment perspective.

Rydex Investments developed the Essential Portfolio Theory (EPT). This presents a dynamic approach to investing. EPT uses active risk management techniques and modern financial instruments, investment strategies that were previously available only to sophisticated institutional investors.

EPT provides traders and investors with investing tenets linked to active risk management and advanced portfolio concepts. These tenets have the potential to create true diversification and maximize returns regardless of market conditions. EPT expands upon the traditional asset allocation choices and considers asset classes both positively and negatively correlated to the market. This includes commodities, futures, real estate, inverse investments, hedge funds, and leveraged or currency securities. Using these may help investors achieve truly diversified portfolios that reduce risk.

EPT examines using leverage to increase exposure to select market indexes. This method can free up assets to invest in alternative asset classes.

Investors and traders should understand, and Rydex research suggests, that long-only portfolios increase in value only in a rising environment. By adding short or inverse financial securities to their portfolios, traders and investors can potentially reduce market risks.

Rydex Investments also advocates moving away from cap weighting. Cap-weighted strategies are equivalent to a buy-and-hold strategy in that the largest companies play a major role in performance. By moving to an equal-weight-based strategy, where an investment is equally divided among the stocks in its index and continually rebalanced to maintain its equal weight, investors enjoy a broad, dynamic exposure to an index.

SHORTCOMINGS IN THE MODERN PORTFOLIO THEORY OF INVESTING

In its research, Essential Portfolio Theory (EPT) reveals differences between itself and Modern Portfolio Theory (MPT). EPT agrees with certain provisions of MPT, but also notes that there are many more investment tools today than when MPT was developed. This increase in the number of tools gives investors and traders many more choices.

Basically, MPT advocates allocating between stocks, bonds, and cash, depending on the risk tolerance and investment objective of the investor.

Critics of MPT say it was created by economists, who try to understand the market as a whole, rather than business analysts, who ascertain what makes each investment opportunity unique. MPT advocates describe investments in terms of their expected long-term return rate and their expected short-term volatility. The goal in MPT is to identify an investor's or trader's acceptable level of risk tolerance, and construct a portfolio with the maximum expected return for that level of risk.

RYDEX S&P EQUAL WEIGHT ETF

One of the newest tools used by Rydex Investments is the different weighting given to indexes. This choice of weighting allows market participants to move away from only cap weighting. Prior to Rydex's white paper regarding EPT, virtually all benchmarks were cap-weighted structured equity portfolios.

Rydex Investment's first ETF was the Rydex S&P Equal Weight ETF (symbol RSP). RSP attempts to replicate the performance of the S&P Equal Weight Index before expenses and fees—an index that Standard & Poor's and Rydex developed. The index rebalances quarterly to maintain its equal weight structure.

The ETF has performed well. From its inception in April 2003 through June 2007, the ETF would have returned about $22,000 versus about $18,000 for the S&P 500 Index. This return includes reinvestment of dividends and capital gains, but does not include fees or expenses.

The ETF attempts to get broad exposure to all the companies comprising the S&P 500 Index, but without a small group of stocks dominating the ETF. The equal-weighting formula also attempts to eliminate the large company bias in the S&P 500 Index. The ETF is broadly diversified, with 4.80 percent in Insurance; 3.92 percent in Oil, Gas, and Consumable Fuels; 3.85 percent in Semiconductors and Semiconductor Equipment; 3.78 percent in Commercial banks; 3.41 percent in Media; 3.38 percent in Specialty Retail; 3.21 percent in Health Care Providers and Services; and other sectors.

RSP was the first noncap-weighted, nonprice-weighted benchmark. It proved that equal weighting or other types of weighting that required more frequent rebalancing can work especially well in an ETF structure.

PAST LIMITATION OF THE MUTUAL FUND STRUCTURE

Some of the initial indexes were equal weighted. Actually, the world's first index fund, developed by Wells Fargo for Samsonite Corporation, was equally weighted. But putting equal weighting in a mutual fund or an investment separate account was expensive.

There were significant transaction costs in taxable accounts, which would detract from performance. There were also tax issues. When rebalancing was done every quarter, gains or losses would have to be taken.

Because of these factors, only equal-weighted indexes could be used efficiently in a qualified account. A qualified account is tax sheltered, such as a profit sharing or pension account. The taxes are paid in these accounts at a later date. Mutual funds were not built to have frequent rebalancing, which is what equal-weighted indexes have to do. Mutual funds lent themselves more to cap-weighted structures.

Because of the unique features of the ETF structure, such as trading on the exchanges, and the ability to create and redeem in a tax-efficient way, the tax exposure can be managed to the point where taxes are not a significant factor. Also, transaction costs can be kept at a manageable level. The S&P Equal Weight Index and RSP were born out of the ETF development. This successful development opened the door for other ETFs to come to market. Shortly after RSP was launched and successful, PWO and PWC from PowerShares came to market. These ETFs also do frequent rebalancing, and they needed the ETF structure in order to be effective.

About two years later, market traders and investors could see that these sorts of ETFs worked—in fact, some of them were outperforming the first ETF generation. This allowed new quantitative ETFs to come to market, broadening the industry away from pure indexing and cap-weighted ETFs.

At that time, there was some controversy that RSP only performed well because the mid-cap value class had performed well. The argument reasoned that since RSP was equally weighted, it had a large exposure to that asset class, and that exposure was skewing its performance records. It also became an in-favor ETF, and RSP was looked on as a way to invest and trade in the small- and mid-cap-size market segment. There was concern, however, that RSP would underperform if large-cap stocks came back into favor.

THE EFFECT OF EQUAL WEIGHT EXPOSURE TO THE CAP-SIZE MARKET SEGMENT

In cap-weighted indexes, bigger companies have more weight in the index than smaller ones, so a price change in the bigger companies will significantly affect the index. In an equal-weighted index, price change in big-cap companies have a limited impact because every company has the same weight and affects the index by the same amount.

A benefit could be that small- and mid-cap stocks can have an impact on the index. Small- and mid-cap stocks historically perform better than large-cap stocks. An equal-weighted index could outperform the market-cap weighted index in the long term.

Rydex has benefited from using its equal weighting method. It uses S&P indexes because S&P is the primary provider of its type of index. This type determines what the U.S. economy looks like and develops this economy snapshot into a benchmark. (The S&P 500 Index is the most commonly known economy snapshot benchmark.)

Rydex uses this S&P approach and attempts to diversify market exposure by moving away from cap weighting. In its sector equal-weighted series, it weights the companies in the S&P sectors equally.

If a strong momentum-based market occurs, large-cap stocks could outperform. In this case RSP will underperform the cap-weighted ETFs.

STOCK PICKERS GRAVITATE TO RSP

When RSP first came out, many stock investors and traders gravitated to the ETF because they liked its makeup. They saw that there was a resemblance between it and their own portfolios. Many of these market people had converted their portfolios closer to equal-weighted compositions than cap-weighted compositions. With RSP's launch and success, they realized they could buy one single security and have market exposure the way they wanted, rather than having to buy many individual stocks.

RSP was created to help in another strategy for stock pickers and traders when they anticipated a break in the market. When they anticipated a broad market decline, they could consider shorting RSP. This would give them participation in a broad market drop that would affect all cap sizes. An equal-weighted ETF such as RSP, because all cap sizes have the same weight, could more accurately replicate a broad market drop.

THE RUSSELL TOP 50 ETF

After RSP was launched it was performing well, and small- and mid-cap stocks, which have equal weighting in the ETF, were expected to continue their good performance. At that time there was no push to develop mega-cap ETFs. For instance, nobody expected the Dow Jones Industrial Index ETF (DIA), to perform well, but DIA broke out on the upside.

Rydex wanted to have a big-cap strategy ETF, and considered different indexes. It decided to offer an ETF that would attempt to replicate the performance of the Russell Top 50 Index. The Russell Top 50 Index ETF (symbol XLG) came out a few years after RSP. After RSP worked well, Rydex was ready to try other ETFs.

Rydex used a mega-large-cap ETF because very large companies had underperformed small and medium caps. Many pundits were looking for some sort of catch-up by big stocks. Rydex wanted an ETF to fill that space.

XLG attempts to replicate the daily investment returns corresponding to the performance of the Russell Top 50 Index. XLG gives cap-weighted exposure to the 50 largest U.S. companies. This weighting allows exposure to over 40 percent of the total market cap of the Russell 3000 Index stock components.

An investor or trader could complement smaller-cap ETFs with a mega-cap ETF that could round out an asset allocation strategy. XLG provides the opportunity to capitalize on short- or intermediate-term large-cap bull market rallies.

The top sector weights are Pharmaceuticals, at 10.67 percent; Oil, Gas, and Consumable Fuels, 10.24 percent; Diversified Financial Services, 8.88 percent; Multi-Utilities, 7.22 percent; Utilities, 6.80 percent; Banks, 6.79 percent; and Computers and Peripherals, 5.98 percent. Other sectors are represented in smaller amounts.

XLG and RSP were the beginning of Rydex's entry into the ETF development space. ETF usage seemed a natural outgrowth of Rydex's Essential Portfolio Theory, allowing it to offer securities such as equal-weighted index securities.

RYDEX STYLE ETFS

At the end of 2005, Standard and Poor's changed their methodology on ranking style, and moved from a 50 percent/50 percent split on the style designation allocated to their indexes. S&P moved to a designation that would allow for some overlap between growth and style designations. It created "pure growth" and a "pure value" style designations. The formulas used to create these designations contained the factors that would ensure that there was no overlap between growth stocks and value stocks.

At this time Rydex wanted to develop style ETFs, to allow traders and investors to participate in this security classification. Rydex set up ETFs to allow traders and investors to participate in pure style exposure. It offers six ETFs, which seek to replicate, before expenses and fees, the performance of the S&P/Citigroup Pure Growth and Pure Value Indexes.

The ETFs offered are Rydex S&P 500 Pure Value ETF, Rydex S&P 500 Pure Growth ETF, Rydex S&P MidCap 400 Pure Value

ETF, Rydex S&P MidCap 400 Pure Growth ETF, Rydex S&P Small-Cap 600 Pure Value ETF, and Rydex S&P SmallCap 600 Pure Growth ETF.

The S&P/Citigroup Style Indexes offer indexes that do more than consider only a single variable such as price to book. Instead, there are three growth variables: the five-year historical earnings per share growth rate, the five-year historical sales per share growth rate, and the five-year average annual internal growth rate. Four variables are used to classify companies as value: the book to price ratio, the sales to price ratio, the cash flow to price ratio, and the dividend yield.

Stocks in the index are eliminated in structuring the pure value and pure growth series. The stocks eliminated are those that do not fit into a pure value or pure growth category. Eliminating these stocks keeps the style series pure.

The amount of stocks comprising the ETFs can vary. For instance, there are 112 stocks in the Rydex S&P MidCap 400 Pure Value ETF (symbol RFV). There are fewer than 400 value and growth stocks in the Rydex pure style ETFs.

The reason for this is that about one-third of the stocks in the S&P MidCap 400 Index will be pure value, about one-third will be pure growth, and about one-third will be dropped from the S&P MidCap 400 Pure Style Index because those stocks will not be "pure" enough to fit into either style. (In the Rydex style score weighting, no security can comprise over 2 percent of an index.)

RYDEX EQUAL WEIGHT SECTOR ETFs

These ETFs seek to replicate as closely as possible, before expenses, the performance of an S&P Equal Weight Index sector. The Rydex Equal Weight Sector strategy is basically a carve-out of the strategy that went into designing RSP: the equal-weighted S&P 500 ETF. Rydex analyzed the S&P Global (GIC) Sectors and broke them out into equal-weighted indexes, and in turn created ETFs to attempt to replicate their performances.

S&P Global Sector Indexes represent the opportunity set of investable equities based on their Global Industry Classification Standard's (GICS) 10 Sectors. These indexes are designed to offer diversification as well as opportunities to benefit from exposure to specific sectors as determined by S&P.

In the Rydex arrangement, however, because the Telecom sector is so small (comprised of only 12 stocks), the sector is rolled into the utility sector. Telecom stocks look and act much like utility stocks, in Rydex's view. The people who buy telecom stocks buy them much for the same reason they buy utility stocks. Therefore the Rydex equal-weighted sector universe is comprised of nine sectors.

THE RYDEX EQUAL-WEIGHTED TECHNOLOGY SECTOR ETF

The Rydex Equal-Weighted Technology Sector ETF (symbol RYT) affords exposure to one of the leading sectors of many market advances: the IT sector. Unlike many of the other IT sector ETFs, which are cap weighted, RYT gives equal weighting to each company in the index, no matter the market cap size of the company.

The difference between a cap-weighted ETF and RYT is that a cap-weighted ETF will usually have a large percentage of its portfolio in a small number of big-cap stocks. In an equal-weighted ETF such as RYT, there is no overexposure to large- and meg-cap stocks.

For representation in the IT sector, for instance, you could buy QQQQ, which would give you exposure to mostly big-cap IT stocks. If you thought the advance would be broad based, with small- and mid-cap stocks leading the advance, RYT would be the better choice, giving you broad exposure to that sector.

KEEPING THE CREATION AND REDEMPTION PROCESS TAX EFFICIENT

ETF managers want to have the fewest capital gains events they can manage, and they also want to match their benchmark indexes. With 1940 Act ETFs, managers are trying to match their benchmarks, not beat them.

There are problems in beating the benchmark index. There are traders shorting an ETF, thinking that the benchmark will decline. Beating the index might keep the shorts from having the performance they deserve. Shorts would prefer the manager underperform an index. But underperforming would not be fair to the ETF holder.

An ETF contains a number of stocks in its portfolio. For example, an S&P 500 ETF will contain 500 stocks. Generally, when an ETF portfolio manager buys stocks, the price of the stocks is not that important from a creation-cost basis. Of course the manager wants to get the best price for the portfolios, but whatever the price, what the ETF pays for stocks becomes its cost basis for that creation unit.

However, when portfolio managers sell stocks in the redemption process, they are sensitive to the price of the stocks they sell. Ordinarily they do not want to sell stocks in which there will be a significant capital-gains event, if they can avoid it. The highest-cost stock will usually be sold for redemptions, so that the lowest capital gains will have to be taken by the ETF.

There are ways to work around capital-gains events. The manager could hold the low-priced stocks and sell other stocks. This is not always an option, however, since a portfolio might have only low-priced stock to sell. The manager could ask a specialist or a market maker if either one had ETF shares that they were holding for trading purposes, and that they might want to sell. If they would sell to the ETF maker, the maker could buy the ETFs and not have to sell shares to start a redemption process.

If the manager thinks the most prudent course is to sell low-priced shares, he or she would do that and book the capital gains. Throughout the year the manager would attempt to sell some higher-priced shares in the redemption process and take a loss, which the manager could book against a previously taken gain.

These strategies can be used for all ETFs. They are much more complex to implement with those ETFs that have a large amount of annual turnover, such as fundamentally weighted ETFs, equally weighted ETFs, and other intelligent ETFs

RESULTS OF THE RSP CREATION AND REDEMPTION PROCESS

The S&P 500 Equal Weight ETF (RSP) was five years old in April 2008. Its annualized gain over that time is better than the S&P 500 Index. On an annualized basis, RSP has about a 40 percent stock turnover.

With that good performance and high amount of turnover, RSP has taken no capital gain that it has had to pass on to holders. RSP has also accumulated in this time a realized capital loss, which can be used in the future against any realized capital gain. What drives this efficiency is the creation and redemption ETF process. Whenever there are redemptions, RSP attempts to divest itself of lower-cost basis stocks in a tax-efficient way.

Chapter | 6

PROSHARES

The 20-year bull market ended in the early 2000s, and many traders and investors are more sophisticated and demanding now, wanting more than a basic asset allocation strategy. Instead of plain vanilla representation in markets and market segments, they are looking for ways to gain alpha in lower-volatility global markets.

Index investing through ETFs has moved well beyond index investing as it was known throughout the 1980s and 1990s. Today's markets are very different. During the years when the markets, especially the technology sector, were appreciating 15 to 20 percent, people started to expect those returns. But that number is much more than the S&P 500 Index of 10.46 percent a year, and recent markets are going back to the historical average gain or lower.

INDEXING IS FILLING A NEED

Indexing will continue to grow. According to numbers coming from various securities industries sources, index securities classes now account for about 30 percent of annual cash flows in mutual funds. For equity assets that are invested in index funds and ETFs, that amount is about 22 percent and is increasing.

There is an opportunity for traders and investors to find mis-valuations in the various asset classes and market segments, and to buy or short to take advantage of those differences. Adding even a 10 to 20 percent magnified posture in a portfolio can enhance those returns, which can be very important in the present and expected lower-volatility market environment.

This is where ProShares comes in. ProShares is a creator of ETFs, and each of its ETFs tracks a popular index. But it is not a traditional ETF creator, and it takes the concept of indexing one step further. ProShares ETFs seek daily investment results, before fees and expenses, that correspond to an index. Its Ultra ETFs seek magnified results of an index. The Ultra ETFs magnify the daily performance of an index, seeking to get performance exposure for less cash invested, therefore adding alpha. Of course, the risk is also magnified.

On the short side of the market, ProShares offers a series of inverse funds that seeks daily investment results, before fees and expenses, that correspond to the inverse (opposite) of the daily performance of an index.

ADVANTAGES OF PROSHARES

The inverse ProShares have advantages over using a margin account when shorting the market. With ProShares your loss is limited to the amount of your investment. In a margin account you can incur margin calls, you have to maintain a minimum equity in the account, and when the equity is not sufficient, you will receive more margin calls. Also, if you have an IRA account you cannot short the market, since short positions can only be done in a margin account, and IRAs cannot be margin accounts. You can accomplish a short market position with ProShares, since they can be purchased in an IRA. Also, in a margin account you must pay interest on the amount of funds you are borrowing. This interest is paid monthly, and the amount of interest is usually higher than the prime rate.

ProShares inverse ETFs can be used to take advantage of a negative view of the markets, including broad general market indexes and market segments. Also, inverse ETFs can be important hedging tools. If investors or traders are nervous about the market and want to cut down on risk but not take profits (perhaps because they think there will be a rebound shortly or there is a tax consequence they want to avoid), they can use inverse ETFs to adjust or neutralize market exposure.

These techniques are used frequently by hedge funds. You can create your own hedging techniques cheaply and easily using inverse ETFs. As tools for implementing a market position or adjusting volatility, you can accomplish some interesting strategies using inverse ETFs.

THE CHANGING ROLE OF ETFs

First there were ETFs that allowed indexing through tracking broad indexes such as the S&P 500 and the Nasdaq 100 indexes. The next wave of indexing attempts to add alpha to a portfolio, while still using basic asset allocation through sector and other indexes. With the growth of sector ETFs, traders and investors can take advantage of mis-valuations that occur in sectors that comprise the broad-based indexes.

An interesting addition, although riskier, is the potential in the alpha-seeking magnified sector ETFs. By buying one of the new magnified ETFs offered by ProShares, investors and traders can gain alpha on the long side by increasing the buying power of their capital with magnified exposure, take a short position, or hedge gains in other investments with short exposure.

INCREASING EXPOSURE THROUGH PROSHARES

Here is a simple example of how this works. Say you have a $50,000 equity portfolio, you think the market is about to climb, and you want more exposure. You could sell $10,000 of your present equities and buy one of the magnified ETFs. You would then have $40,000 in equities and $10,000 in a magnified ETF. The magnified ETF will give you about $20,000 worth of exposure, which gives you about a $60,000 market exposure overall.

You have increased your market exposure by about 20 percent. This is what many hedge funds do; when they think the market will advance, they use leverage. Of course, you have also increased your risk.

That is one thing you can accomplish with magnified ETFs. The magnified funds seek daily investment results, before fees and expenses, that correspond to a multiple, such as one and a half or two times (200 percent) the daily performance of the index it tracks. If you buy a magnified ETF on the S&P 500, for example, for each 1 percent a day that the S&P 500 advances, the ETF is structured to advance about 2 percent a day. If you buy a magnified inverse ETF, for each 1 percent a day the S&P 500 declines, the inverse ETF will attempt to advance about 2 percent a day. Of course, your risk is magnified also. If you buy an inverse magnified Nasdaq 100 ETF and the Nasdaq 100 index goes up 1 percent a day, you will have about a 2 percent decline a day in your magnified ETF.

Sector magnified ETFs are also available. When you decide a sector is under- or overvalued, you can buy or short that sector using a sector ETF. If you wish to take a more aggressive stance, you can buy or short a sector using a magnified ETF, which will enhance your return if you are right.

However, traders or investors can manage their degrees of risk. Using magnified ETFs they can magnify their exposure by 10 or 20 percent or whatever they decide they want as a percentage of their portfolio, keeping their risk more manageable.

GAINING DIVERSIFICATION USING PROSHARES

The investors or traders can add volatility to their overall market strategy. With a magnified 200 percent ETF, you will get about twice the return per day that you would get in an ETF that is not magnified. You will not get a full 200 percent return because there are expenses and fees that will reduce your return. Over the long term the ETF will not return exactly 200 percent, although it is magnified two to one.

With magnified ETFs you get more representation for fewer dollars invested. You can, therefore, use the dollars that are freed up to get more diversification by buying sectors or market segments that are not as correlated to your major portfolio position. This diversification could act to lower portfolio risk.

By magnifying your market position with magnified ETFs, although you might be increasing diversification, you are also increasing overall risk. Never think that you will have less overall market risk by diversifying; in fact, you will have more risk because of your magnified overall position.

USING MAGNIFIED ETFs FOR SECTOR DIVERSIFICATION

For example, say that you have $100,000 to invest (the same principle applies if you have $5,000, $10,000, or any amount). You could invest that $100,000 into SPY or IVV or another S&P 500 Index ETF and have broad-based market representation. But perhaps you want more market exposure than simply the S&P 500 Index. Say you want additional exposure to oil and gas. With that same $100,000 you could buy $50,000 worth of SSO, which is the ProShares magnified S&P 500 Index, which seeks daily results corresponding to about twice the daily performance of the S&P 500. With the $50,000 you freed up by using magnified ETFs, you could put $25,000 into DIG, the ProShares Ultra Oil and Gas ETF. This $25,000 gives you nearly a daily 200 percent return exposure to an oil and gas stock index. This exposure is about the same as if you had put $50,000 into an oil and gas index, but with this strategy, you still have $25,000 cash for investing, for fixed-income, or for another strategy.

Depending on how much weight you want in sectors and how much magnified investing you want, or can stomach, you might consider combining strategies. Looking at the above example, you could invest that $50,000 freed up by buying SSO and XLE, which is the Select SPDR Energy Sector ETF. XLE is not a ProShares ETF and is nonmagnified. Investing $50,000 in XLE weights your portfolio in energy, but your return will be less than that possibly attained with DIG. As mentioned, your potential loss would be less also.

Or if you want overweight magnified sector positions in Health Care and Technology, you could buy ROM, the magnified Technology ProShares ETF, and RXL, the magnified Health Care ProShares ETF.

This is an aggressive posture only to be used if your risk profile is appropriate for this strategy.

As shown above, you can control the amount of risk you are taking on. You can magnify your portfolio to what is manageable and desirable for you, maybe taking on a 5 or 10 percent magnified position, depending on your risk profile and risk desire.

SHORTING SECTORS WITH PROSHARES

You can also use inverse ETFs to take the short side of the market or a market segment. For instance, suppose you are long SPY or IVV or another ETF that tracks the S&P 500 Index. And further suppose that you love the broad market representation you are getting but think the energy sector is suspect. The price of oil has climbed to where you think the next move is seriously down. You really do not want to be in that sector.

You could buy the ProShares ETF Ultra Short Oil & Gas Sector (symbol DUG). DUG is not comprised of the same stocks as in that sector of the S&P 500 Index, but it is sector representation and usually sectors move together. The indexes will not move exactly together, but usually in the same direction. So your net position is long oil and gas as part of the S&P 500 Index ETF, and about double short oil and gas through DUG, which attempts to give an inverse approximate 200 percent daily return. This leaves you in a net short position in that sector.

If the energy sector does decline, the price of your inverse ETF will advance, hedging the loss in that position in the S&P 500 Index, and giving you a net gain in the position. You can do the same with technology, health care, or any other sectors that ProShares offers.

MARKET CAP-SIZE HEDGING THROUGH PROSHARES

Through ProShares cap-sizes can also be bought and shorted, magnified and nonmagnified. Say that you are aggressive, know what you are doing, and keep your risks within your risk profile, meaning you can afford to lose the money you are investing or trading. You do not like big-cap stocks and think that segment will go down. You can short the S&P 500 Index, which is basically a big-cap stock index, by buying ProShares inverse S&P 500 Index (symbol SDS). This is an Ultra ETF, and it seeks to return about twice the inverse daily performance of the S&P 500 Index.

At the same time, you love small-cap stocks, and think this segment will grow sharply over the next several years. You could buy SAA, which is the ProShares Ultra Small-Cap 600. This ETF seeks to return about twice the daily performance of that index. This is an aggressive stance and has risk as well as profit potential. If big-cap goes down, the S&P 500 Index should decline, and SDS will advance. SDS, an inverse ETF, should go up at about a 200 percent rate of return of the daily performance of the S&P 500 Index decline. If small-cap stocks advance, the S&P 500 Small-Cap 600 Index should advance also. SAA, a magnified ETF, should perform at about a 200 percent daily rate of return to the Small-Cap Index.

HOW DOES PROSHARES ACHIEVE MAGNIFIED RESULTS?

ProShares states in its disclaimers that it is attempting to, and expects to, achieve its magnified goals, but these objectives are not guaranteed. There is no guarantee that a ProShares security will achieve an approximate 200 percent of the daily performance of its benchmark index when this is its objective. There are risks, including inverse correlation, leverage, market price variance, and short sale risks.

Traditional ETFs buy stocks in the creation process, and each ETF share contains the same proportionate amount of company names that is in the tracked index. ProShares structures its magnified ETFs differently, and might use derivatives in trying to meet its goals. This is not to be confused with some ETFs, especially foreign country ETFs, which use optimized formulas in structuring their securities.

HOW PROSHARES ACHIEVES MAGNIFIED RETURNS

When considering using magnified ETFs, you should have some knowledge of how ProShares achieves its returns. It is always good to know the details of ETFs you trade or invest in. This is especially true regarding magnified securities, which are more volatile and are not for those who do not understand the risk they are taking.

ProShares uses a very simple process to receive returns on their magnified ETFs. It uses a total return swap on the index it is magnifying, which is the derivative equivalent of buying the underlying index.

ProShares normally deals with a swap counterparty. Suppose that the S&P 500 Index is trading at 1500. ProShares would enter into a swap agreement that stipulates that it will buy, for instance, $100 million of the index in a long swap at a price of 1500. This is a long swap, and the following refers to long position swaps. ProShares would pay the counterparty fixed (short-term interest), and the counterparty would pay ProShares floating (the change in the index performance). If the S&P 500 Index went up 15 points, for instance, which is a 1 percent increase, then the counterparty would owe ProShares $1 million. This is because

ProShares has a notional loan with the counterparty, and the counterparty owes ProShares 1 percent of the notional. The term *notional* refers to the face, or amount, of the swap. ProShares would have a $1 million gain because the price of the underlying index went up. If the price of the index declined by 1 percent, ProShares would owe the counterparty $1 million. Remember, this profit or loss is paid by the holder of the magnified security, which is *you* if you buy the security. The value of your investment would go up or down the 1 percent noted.

ProShares follows strict procedures in its leveraging process. It has an internal credit committee. One of its requirements is that the swap counterparties it deals with must be rated A or better. The counterparty must not be an associated party as far as creating or redeeming ETFs, and must be independent from that process. Typically a counterparty is a major bank or large broker-dealer. On long transactions, the counterparty enters into an agreement with ProShares to make the transaction, and typically the agreement includes interest to be paid by ProShares on each transaction.

Probably the counterparty would hedge the position created by the ProShares transaction, but not necessarily. If it is a major brokerage firm, it could hedge by adding the transaction to its hedged book. A bank would probably hedge its transaction at once in the marketplace. *Hedge* means to take a short position versus a long position, and vice versa, therefore balancing out risk while making money on the interest charged to create the position.

COSTS TO THE ETF BUYER

Instead of putting up millions of dollars to participate in an index, ProShares goes to institutions and sets up transactions. This leverage is passed on to ETF buyers and works very well. The costs to use these securities classes are reasonable when considering the value received by the ETF buyers. On a daily basis it is hard to notice the interest paid by ProShares to its counterparties and its special expenses because these expenses are only 1 or 2 basis points a day. This expense is not noticeable as a drag on the performances of its ETFs.

Any time leverage is used, money has to be borrowed, and ProShares has to pay interest for its borrowing. If ProShares used futures contracts or options to manage leverage, ProShares would have to borrow money. The cost is calculated and adjusted into the ETF net asset value, and the amount is so small it is not noticed on a daily basis.

The following ETFs offer a high amount of potential alpha and downside hedge opportunity. The slightly higher costs seem reasonable when considering the strategy options that this unique set of ETFs offers.

SHORT AND ULTRASHORT MARKET CAP

Short QQQ, Symbol PSQ. Seeks daily investment results, before fees and expenses, that correspond to the inverse (opposite) of the daily performance of the Nasdaq 100 Index.

Short S&P500, Symbol SH. Seeks daily investment results, before fees and expenses, that correspond to the inverse (opposite) of the daily performance of the S&P 500 Index.

Short MidCap400, Symbol MYY. Seeks daily investment results, before fees and expenses, that correspond to the inverse (opposite) of the daily performance of the S&P Mid-Cap 400 Index.

Short Dow30, Symbol DOG. Seeks daily investment results, before fees and expenses, that correspond to the inverse (opposite) of the daily performance of the Dow Jones Industrial Average.

Short Russell2000, Symbol RWM. Seeks daily investment results, before fees and expenses, that correspond to the inverse (opposite) of the daily performance of the Russell 2000 index.

Short SmallCap600, Symbol SBB. Seeks daily investment results, before fees and expenses, that correspond to the inverse (opposite) of the daily performance of the S&P Small-Cap 600 Index.

UltraShort QQQ, Symbol QID. Seeks daily investment results, before fees and expenses, that correspond to twice (200 percent) the inverse (opposite) of the daily performance of the Nasdaq 100 Index.

UltraShort S&P500, Symbol SDS. Seeks daily investment results, before fees and expenses, that correspond to twice (200 percent) the inverse (opposite) of the daily performance of the S&P 500 Index.

UltraShort MidCap400, Symbol MVV. Seeks daily investment results, before fees and expenses, that correspond to twice (200 percent) the inverse (opposite) of the daily performance of the S&P Mid-Cap 400 Index.

UltraShort Dow30, Symbol DXD. Seeks daily investment results, before fees and expenses, that correspond to twice (200 percent) the inverse (opposite) of the daily performance of the Dow Jones Industrial Average.

UltraShort Russell2000, Symbol UWM. Seeks daily investment results, before fees and expenses, that correspond to twice (200 percent) the inverse (opposite) of the daily performance of the Russell 2000 Index.

UltraShort SmallCap600, Symbol SDD. Seeks daily investment results, before fees and expenses, that correspond to twice (200 percent) the inverse (opposite) of the daily performance of the S&P Small-Cap 600 Index.

ULTRASHORT STYLE

UltraShort Russell1000 Value, Symbol SJF. Seeks daily investment results, before fees and expenses, that correspond to twice (200 percent) the inverse (opposite) of the daily performance of the Russell 1000 Value Index.

UltraShort Russell1000 Growth, Symbol SFK. Seeks daily investment results, before fees and expenses, that correspond to twice (200 percent) the inverse (opposite) of the daily performance of the Russell 100 Growth Index.

UltraShort Russell MidCap Value, Symbol SJL. Seeks daily investment results, before fees and expenses, that correspond to twice (200 percent) the inverse (opposite) of the daily performance of the Russell Mid-Cap Value Index.

UltraShort Russell MidCap Growth, Symbol SDK. Seeks daily investment results, before fees and expenses, that correspond to twice (200 percent) the inverse (opposite) of the daily performance of the Mid-Cap Growth Index.

UltraShort Russell2000 Value, Symbol SJH. Seeks daily investment results, before fees and expenses, that correspond to twice (200 percent) the inverse (opposite) of the daily performance of the Russell 2000 Value Index.

UltraShort Russell2000 Growth, Symbol SKK. Seeks daily investment results, before fees and expenses, that correspond to twice (200 percent) the inverse (opposite) of the daily performance of the Russell 2000 Growth Index.

ULTRASHORT SECTOR

UltraShort Basic Materials, Symbol SMN. Seeks daily investment results, before fees and expenses, that correspond to twice (200 percent) the inverse (opposite) of the daily performance of the Dow Jones U.S. Basic Materials Index.

UltraShort Consumer Goods, Symbol SZK. Seeks daily investment results, before fees and expenses, that correspond to twice (200 percent) the inverse (opposite) of the daily performance of the Dow Jones U.S. Consumer Goods Index.

UltraShort Consumer Services, Symbol SCC. Seeks daily investment results, before fees and expenses, that correspond to twice (200 percent) of the inverse (opposite) of the daily performance of the Dow Jones Consumer Services Index.

UltraShort Financials, Symbol SKF. Seeks daily investment results, before fees and expenses, that correspond to twice (200 percent) the inverse (opposite) of the daily performance of the Dow Jones U.S. Financial Index.

UltraShort Health Care, Symbol RXD. Seeks daily investment results, before fees and expenses, that correspond to twice (200 percent) the inverse (opposite) of the daily performance of the Dow Jones U.S. Health Care Index.

UltraShort Industrials, Symbol SIJ. Seeks daily investment results, before fees and expenses, that correspond to twice (200 percent) the inverse (opposite) of the daily performance of the Dow Jones U.S. Industrials Index.

UltraShort Oil & Gas, Symbol DUG. Seeks daily investment results, before fees and expenses, that correspond to twice (200 percent) the inverse (opposite) of the daily performance of the Dow Jones U.S. Oil & Gas Index.

UltraShort Real Estate, Symbol SRS. Seeks daily investment results, before fees and expenses, that correspond to twice (200 percent) the inverse (opposite) of the daily performance of the Dow Jones U.S. Real Estate Index.

UltraShort Semiconductors, Symbol SSG. Seeks daily investment results, before fees and expenses, that correspond to twice (200 percent) the inverse (opposite) of the daily performance of the Dow Jones U.S. Semiconductors Index.

UltraShort Technology, Symbol REW. Seeks daily investment results, before fees and expenses, that correspond to twice (200 percent) the inverse (opposite) of the daily performance of the Dow Jones U.S. Technology Index.

UltraShort Utilities, Symbol SDP. Seeks daily investment results, before fees and expenses, that correspond to twice (200 percent) the inverse (opposite) of the daily performance of the Dow Jones U.S. Utilities Index.

ULTRA PROSHARES

Ultra ProShares seeks daily investment results, before fees and expenses, that correspond to twice (200 percent) the daily performance of the Dow Jones Industrial Average.

ULTRA MARKETCAP

Ultra QQQ, Symbol QLD. Seeks daily investment results, before fees and expenses, that correspond to twice (200 percent) the daily performance of the Nasdaq 100 Index.

Ultra S&P500, Symbol SSO. Seeks daily investment results, before fees and expenses, that correspond to twice (200 percent) the daily performance of the S&P 500 Index.

Ultra MidCap400, Symbol MVV. Seeks daily investment results, before fees and expenses, that correspond to twice (200 percent) the daily performance of the S&P Mid-Cap 400 Index.

Ultra Dow30, Symbol DDM. Seeks daily investment results, before fees and expenses, that correspond to twice (200 percent) the daily performance of the Dow Jones Industrial Average.

Ultra Russell2000, Symbol UWM. Seeks daily investment results, before fees and expenses, that correspond to twice (200 percent) the daily performance of the Russell 2000 Index.

Ultra SmallCap600, Symbol SAA. Seeks daily investment results, before fees and expenses, that correspond to twice

(200 percent) the daily performance of the S&P Small-Cap 600 Index.

ULTRA STYLE

Ultra Russell1000 Value, Symbol UVG. Seeks daily investment results, before fees and expenses, that correspond to twice (200 percent) the daily performance of the Russell 1000 Value Index.

Ultra Russell1000 Growth, Symbol UKF. Seeks daily investment results, before fees and expenses, that correspond to twice (200 percent) the daily performance of the Russell 1000 Growth Index.

Ultra Russell Mid-Cap Value, Symbol UVU. Seeks daily investment results, before fees and expenses, that correspond to twice (200 percent) the daily performance of the Russell Mid-Cap Value Index.

Ultra Russell Mid-Cap Growth, Symbol UKW. Seeks daily investment results, before fees and expenses, that correspond to twice (200 percent) the daily performance of the Russell Mid-Cap Growth Index.

Ultra Russell2000 Value, Symbol UVT. Seeks daily investment results, before fees and expenses, that correspond to twice (200 percent) the daily performance of the Russell 2000 Value Index.

Ultra Russell2000 Growth, Symbol UKK. Seeks daily investment results, before fees and expenses, that correspond to twice (200 percent) the daily performance of the Russell 2000 Growth Index.

ULTRA SECTOR

Ultra Basic Materials, Symbol UYM. Seeks daily investment results, before fees and expenses, that correspond to twice (200 percent) the daily performance of the Dow Jones U.S. Basic Materials Index.

Ultra Consumer Goods, Symbol UGE. Seeks daily investment results, before fees and expenses, that correspond to twice (200 percent) the daily performance of the Dow Jones U.S. Consumer Goods Index.

Ultra Consumer Services, Symbol UCC. Seeks daily investment results, before fees and expenses, that correspond to twice (200 percent) the daily performance of the Dow Jones U.S. Consumer Services Index.

Ultra Financials, Symbol UYG. Seeks daily investment results, before fees and expenses, that correspond to twice (200 percent) the daily performance of the Dow Jones U.S. Financial Index.

Ultra Health Care, Symbol RXL. Seeks daily investment results, before fees and expenses, that correspond to twice (200 percent) the daily performance of the Dow Jones U.S. Health Care Index.

Ultra Industrials, Symbol UXI. Seeks daily investment results, before fees and expenses, that correspond to twice (200 percent) the daily performance of the Dow Jones U.S. Industrials Index.

Ultra Oil & Gas, Symbol DIG. Seeks daily investment results, before fees and expenses, that correspond to twice (200 percent) the daily performance of the Dow Jones U.S. Oil & Gas Index.

Ultra Real Estate, Symbol URE. Seeks daily investment
results, before fees and expenses, that correspond to twice
(200 percent) the daily performance of the Dow Jones U.S.
Real Estate Index.

Ultra Semiconductors, Symbol USD. Seeks daily investment
results, before fees and expenses, that correspond to twice
(200 percent) the daily performance of the Dow Jones U.S.
Semiconductors Index.

Ultra Technology, Symbol ROM. Seeks daily investment
results, before fees and expenses, that correspond to twice
(200 percent) the daily performance of the Dow Jones U.S.
Technology Index.

Ultra Utilities, Symbol UPW. Seeks daily investment
results, before fees and expenses, that correspond to twice
(200 percent) the daily performance of the Dow Jones U.S.
Utilities Index.

Chapter | 7

WISDOMTREE

ADVANTAGES OF DIVIDEND-WEIGHTED INDEXES

WisdomTree provides investors and traders with fundamentally weighted ETFs that are designed to track indexes weighted by dividends or earnings. WisdomTree ETFs can serve as dividend-paying investments or as total return investments meant to be core holdings for investors.

Dividend-paying stocks have long had their adherents, but this could be an especially good time for dividend-weighted investing. Adherents cite the fact that many investors and traders in the United States are aging, and therefore these investors will focus on income, or certainly keep it among their mix of interests. Dividends have always provided a large part of the total return in many major indexes. For instance, over 40 percent of the return of the S&P 500 Index from 1926 through 2005 came from dividends. Also, corporations currently have high cash levels, and paying dividends is a good way to make their stock more attractive.

Dividends are attractive to investors on an after-tax basis. Investors are taxed at a 15 percent rate on qualifying dividend income; this rate could go up in the future. This rate was 39 percent before reductions were made in 2003. Dividends show transparency, and after debacles such as Enron and WorldCom, investors and traders are demanding to know the truth about the earnings of the companies in which they are investing.

Jeremy J. Siegel, professor of finance at the Wharton School of University of Pennsylvania, is one of the believers in the dividend-weighted indexing approach. As a Senior Investment Strategy Advisor to WisdomTree and a member of WisdomTree's board of directors, he opines there are better ways to construct indexes than the cap-weighted indexing method. In an article he wrote for the *Wall Street Journal* ("The Noisy Market Hypothesis," June 14, 2006), Professor Siegel points out that stock prices are influenced by speculators and momentum traders, and this affects company valuations as much or more than any other factor. Stock prices are affected, especially in the short term, by rumors or nonimportant events mixed in with important information. This information is then randomly over- or under-emphasized by traders, brokers, and other market participants. He calls these stock-price-moving factors "noise," and believes this creates short-term over- and undervaluations.

Professor Siegel has long advocated for stock evaluation using dividends as the main focus. One of his reasons is that dividends cannot be manipulated by corporate management; if the money is not there, dividends cannot be paid. After corporate fiascos of the past, investors are saying, "Show me the money," which is what dividends do.

Dividend-weighted portfolios have the potential of being especially beneficial in bear markets. The Russell 3000 Index lost a substantial amount of its value between March 2000 and the bear market low in October 2002. It is reported that some dividend-weighted indexes had a much better performance than this. There are many ways to fundamentally weight indexes, and dividend weighting is one of the ways. Evidence suggests that weighting by dividends has distinct advantages over other weighting strategies.

TRANSPARENCY OF CASH DIVIDENDS

There is some disagreement among index creators about which is the most accurate indicator of the fundamental value of a company: dividends or earnings. Earnings can profitably be reinvested in the company if not paid out as dividends, some argue, and as earnings grow that will make possible future higher earnings and future higher dividends.

WisdomTree used dividends as its primary weighting factor for several reasons. A cash dividend is an objective measure, and management cannot hide earnings' shortcomings when they pay a cash dividend. Also, a company's cash flow can be interpreted in many ways, whereas dividends are specific, and no interpretation is more direct than payment of cash. Dividend payments from a company are rarely thought of as negative indications of a company's operations and prospects. Therefore, dividend payments or lack of them can reflect opinions of management and executives about the future of a company.

CRITERIA FOR DIVIDEND-WEIGHTED INDEX INCLUSION

To be eligible for inclusion in a domestic WisdomTree Dividend Index, a company must meet set criteria. A company must pay a regular dividend. The company stock must be common shares or real estate investment trust (REIT) shares. The company's market capitalization must be at least $100 million, and the average daily dollar trading volume must be $100,000 or more. The company must be incorporated in the United States, which means American Depositary Receipts (ADRs) do not qualify. The stock must be traded on the NYSE, AMEX, or Nasdaq market.

In domestic indexes, the high-yielding indexes are created by selecting the top 30 percent of all stocks in the WisdomTree Dividend Index with market caps of at least $200 million and average daily trading volume of at least $200,000 over the preceding three months.

For international indexes, the weighting methodology is identical to the domestic index requirements with some additional requirements. The international WisdomTree companies must be incorporated in one of the 21 developed equity markets, and each company must have paid at least $5 million in cash dividends in the prior years. Non-U.S. securities must list their shares on a major non-U.S. stock exchange. Such shares must have traded at least 250,000 shares per month for the six months prior to the screening period.

WISDOMTREE: INDEX CREATOR AND ETF SPONSOR

What makes WisdomTree unusual is that it is both an index creator and an ETF sponsor. It has the ability to create indexes and can subsequently launch ETFs that track their created indexes. WisdomTree indexes, which its ETFs seek to replicate, are fundamentally weighted, and constructed to give broad market exposure. This is the way traditional passive indexes, such as the original ETF generation, were designed to work. Instead of being constructed in a cap-weighted structure, WisdomTree's fundamentally weighted indexes are weighted either by its component companies' dividend streams or their earnings.

WisdomTree started out with 30 dividend-weighted indexes and in February 2007 launched six earnings-weighted indexes. The dividend indexes capture all of the dividend-paying companies and weights the indexes according to the cash dividends paid by those companies. The earnings ETFs weight according to a company's earnings.

WisdomTree is a passive index provider, and its broad, size-based indexes are created by selecting stocks based on any sort of quantitative analysis. Stocks are put into the indexes based simply on the amount of dividends they pay or the earnings produced.

WisdomTree reconstitutes its indexes once a year. For domestic indexes this occurs in December; international index reconstituting is done in June. Dividends from the domestic WisdomTree ETFs are paid to the ETF holder quarterly; international dividends are paid to the holder yearly in December.

INTERNATIONAL AND DOMESTIC DIVIDEND INDEXING

There is an advantage to diversifying internationally. As part of a broad asset allocation, investors should have some international exposure. Studies suggest investors are increasing this representation and searching for the best way to get exposure. The advantages of investing internationally include geographic diversification, higher returns potential, and the potential for lower volatility. WisdomTree espouses that dividend stream–weighting may be a more intelligent approach when investing internationally.

For historical perspective, consider the Morgan Stanley Capital International Europe, Australasia, and Far East (MSCI EAFE) index. At the top of the Japanese stock market bubble, the Japanese market comprised about 70 percent of the MSCI EAFE index. This was because the huge Japanese stock market gain caused many Japanese stocks to have huge market capitalizations, so they were heavily weighted in the index.

When the Japanese market imploded, it created a decades-long deflation that created a drag on the returns of the EAFE index. If one had simply bought the companies in proportion to their contribution to the international dividend stream, one would have returns better than those generated by the EAFE index from 1996 to 2006.

Investors and traders can receive this exposure by buying WisdomTree ETFs, which set initial weights based on the cash dividends that companies pay, rather than according to a company's market cap.

Look at Figure 7.1. It shows the hypothetical performance of the WisdomTree Japan Index against its benchmark, the MSCI Japan Index. WisdomTree has a Japan ETF (symbol DXJ).

Dividend yields in many parts of the developed world are higher than they are in the United States. This translates into higher gross dividend yields for many international indexes compared to domestic indexes. WisdomTree's international dividend-based ETFs are designed to replicate the daily performances of their indexes. These indexes give greater weight to dividend-paying companies in the United Kingdom, Europe, Australia, and Asia than a comparable cap-weighted index might.

Figure 7.1

WT Japan Dividend Index versus MSCI Japan Index

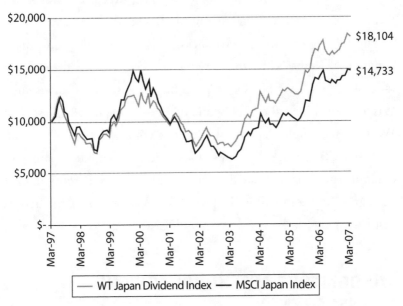

Source: WisdomTree

The WisdomTree DEFA Index measures the performance of dividend-paying companies in the same 21 equity markets covered by the MSCI EAFE Index. The coverage is the same, but the companies in the WisdomTree index are weighted by each company's contribution to the dividend stream of that region.

The yield on the WisdomTree DEFA Index was 4.17 percent as of May 13, 2008, which is generally higher than the yields found in U.S. indexes. One of the most commonly known benchmarks in the United States, the S&P 500 Index, yielded only about 1.7 percent in 2007. The quoted yields relate to the indexes, not for the ETFs that have been created to replicate performances of the indexes. Many of the ETFs have not been out long enough to receive a full year's dividend, so no yearly dividend rate can be stated.

The ETF holder will receive dividends paid from the constituent companies less the ETF expenses and fees. For instance, the expense ratio of the DEFA ETF is 0.48 percent. Expense ratios vary among WisdomTree ETFs; these ratios and other information can be seen at WisdomTree's Web site, www.wisdomtree.com.

WisdomTree research shows that there are many companies in emerging markets that pay dividends, and that an emerging market strategy is very compelling. In July 2007, WisdomTree launched its first Emerging Markets ETF (symbol DEM).

WISDOMTREE METHODOLOGY AND TRANSPARENCY

The ETF structure is used because it is an easily tradable "mirror" to reflect the unique and thorough characteristics of the WisdomTree indexing methodology. These ETFs are designed to replicate the daily returns, before fees and expenses, from its underlying indexes.

In its index construction WisdomTree takes factors into account that make sure its indexes are representative of the market segment they are targeting. WisdomTree ensures its indexes are investable, meaning they contain stocks that can be bought and sold quickly and near their market prices. And probably most important, it constructs indexes with possibilities of good returns, while also considering how much risk is necessary to receive those potential returns.

For more information on WisdomTree's methodology and to see its ETF offerings, go to its Web site www.wisdomtree.com.

INTERNATIONAL WISDOMTREE RETURNS

The highest available yields are generally available in non-U.S. regions. Foreign companies pay higher dividends than U.S. companies, which is why U.S. investors tend to invest in foreign markets when looking for dividends as part of their total return.

The WisdomTree international indexes usually generate excess total hypothetical returns relative to the regional MSCI indexes of EAFE, Europe, and the Pacific Rim ex-Japan for the term periods covered by WisdomTree's back tests.

Look at Figure 7.2.

Figure 7.2

WisdomTree Pacific ex-Japan High-Yielding Equity Index vs. MSCI Pacific ex-Japan Value Index

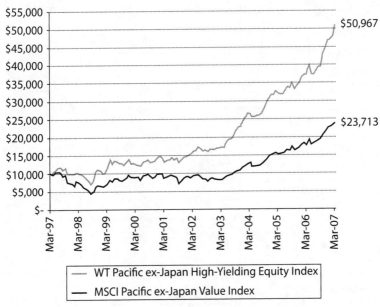

Source: WisdomTree

Figure 7.2 shows the hypothetical results of the WisdomTree Pacific ex-Japan High-Yielding Equity Index versus its benchmark index. The WisdomTree ETF (symbol DNH), attempts to replicate the performance, before fees and expenses, of this index.

Figure 7.3 shows the hypothetical results of the WisdomTree Europe High-Yielding Equity Index versus its benchmark index. The WisdomTree ETF (symbol DEW) attempts to replicate, before fees and expenses, the performance of this index.

Another example is Figure 7.4. It shows the hypothetical results of the WisdomTree DEFA High-Yielding Equity Index versus its benchmark index. The WisdomTree ETF (symbol DTH) attempts to replicate the performance of this index, before fees and expenses.

Figure 7.3

WT Europe High-Yielding Equity Index vs. MSCI Europe Value Index

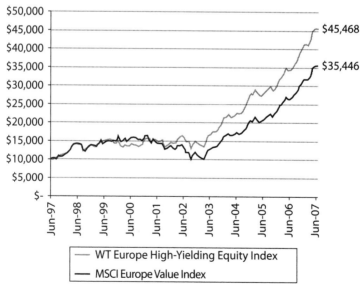

Source: WisdomTree

Figure 7.4

WT DEFA High-Yielding Equity Index vs. MSCI EAFE Value Index

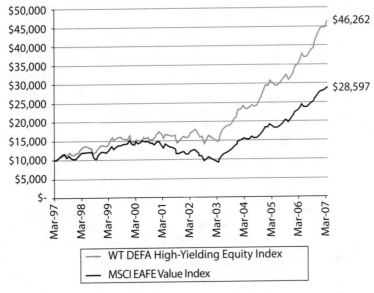

Source: WisdomTree

Chapter | 8

THE ORIGIN AND GROWTH
OF INTELLIGENT ETFs

Changing times call for changing investment options, and the increasing variety of securities that are being packaged as ETFs answers these needs. Modern investing and trading call for continuous development, and ETFs allow for this. ETFs have become a delivery vehicle for quality investment management. Since they are set up to replicate an index that accomplishes specific tasks and exposure, ETFs are passive in that they will go in the general direction of the market but with the unique twists of their index construction.

The variety and types of ETFs being offered are important to understand because they answer the core question of why intelligent ETFs have come into existence.

Enhanced and strategy indexes have been around for some time. Indexing purists have maintained from the start that a sector or industry group is not a pure benchmark, which should be a cap-weighted, broad-market exposure type of index.

A wide variety of indexes have been offered over the years even before ETFs. There were industry group indexes developed for the options exchanges, such as the Philadelphia Options Exchange (PHLX), and the AMEX. These exchanges had equally weighted industry group indexes and other choices, which were a very different type of approach to securities classes than those offered before.

THE ROLE OF THE AMERICAN STOCK EXCHANGE (AMEX) IN THE ETF REVOLUTION

The AMEX is an industry leader in ETF listings with over $300 billion in assets under management that is spread over 208 ETFs. The AMEX is the only primary exchange offering trading across a full range of securities, including ETFs, options, equities, structured securities, and HOLDRS. The AMEX brought the first ETF to market in 1993. The AMEX is a major options exchange, trading options on indexes as well as domestic and foreign stocks.

THE START OF THE INTELLIGENT REVOLUTION

In 2003, after a disastrous bear cycle, in about the same week, Rydex Global Advisors launched the S&P 500 Equal Weight ETF (symbol RSP), and PowerShares launched its first two ETFs, which are based on the Intellidex Index (symbols PWO and PWC). The differences in these two ETF makers reflect the securities classes they offer, and show that intelligent ETFs can have very different approaches. In these cases RSP uses a weighting approach, and PWO and PWC use a selection and weighting approach.

In the new generation of ETFs, the makers offer a large number of different strategies in their securities classes. Some are straightforward access types of strategies, perhaps focusing on a narrow group or an industry that has certain merit. Perhaps a maker is devising an ETF on a timing basis, or maybe devising an ETF for an industry that is difficult to define, such as the alternative energy industry or the water industry. A maker could collect related industries and make an ETF that weaves them all together.

There are also ETFs that are more selection based. Whether the ETF is considering quantitative models or a simple strategy, or using an earnings or dividend model to quantify the selected companies to put into the ETF, there are now offerings that are more varied and fit into a specialized market.

Some of the ETF offerings that are replicating quantitative formulas could be considered sort of a "Dogs of the Dow" on steroids approach. The idea of taking an index and quantifying it has been around for a long time. This is now tied in with the acceptance and growth of the use of ETFs.

ETFs as investment vehicles first became accepted on standard, well-known indexes like the S&P 500 Index and S&P Sector Indexes. These offerings were aimed toward individual investors and traders, and also institutional investors like pension plans and money managers.

ETF providers started realizing that the ETF structure was a perfect way to package indexes, and the indexes could include the alpha-seeking and bear market–resistant types. As an example, the AMEX has an index called the AMEX Institutional Index. It has been in existence since the 1980s, and once had options traded based on its movement. The index was based on stock filings with the SEC that were made by institutional investment managers. Other strategies have been available for decades. The Dogs of the Dow strategy has been in existence since the 1970s.

There have been other quantitative processes applied to select baskets of stocks. These have led to other structured products such as Unit Investment Trusts (UITs), indexing notes, and basket-linked notes.

The indexing niches and alpha-seeking index ideas have been in existence for many years. The ETFs, however, are a new product, and are very well suited to use as packages for indexing methods. They can be traded easily by a wide range of people, from those who have a few thousand dollars to invest to professionals that invest millions of dollars.

The ETF structure is *itself* intelligent. Add to that the evolution of ETF makers who are using intelligent indexes, and there is a double degree of investment capability and potential that is new to the investing public.

THE CHANGING ETF SCENE

ETFs are no longer only a way to mirror the performance of the S&P 500 Index or to replicate the performance of an S&P 500 Index sector. ETFs are now a securities class category, with almost 650 different ETFs being offered, amounting to about $620 billion being invested in the securities class.

The idea that all ETFs can be categorized by one set of characteristics is gone. There are now variations in the exposures that ETFs are trying to deliver. There are ETFs based on asset classes, industry classes, and many other classes. There are also variations of exposure from a long or short or leveraged perspective (see Chapter 6). The increased variety of the indexes involved has increased the benchmarks to those indexes. Leveraged and inverse securities are also having a positive impact of growth in the ETF universe.

MODIFIED CAP-WEIGHTED INDEXES AND SPECIALIZED ETFs

Modified cap-weighted index methods have been used since 1998 and started with the S&P 500 Sector SPDR Index series. There is no one formula for modified cap-weighting methods; there is a variety of methods used to construct these indexing structures. Within each index there is a stated method for how it is to be modified, and this method can be found in the index prospectus.

Some of the most popular indexes that ETFs attempt to replicate are modified cap-weighted. For example, the Nasdaq 100 Index, one of the most used indexes, was changed to a modified weighting before its ETF, QQQQ, was released.

MODIFIED CAP-WEIGHTING METHODS

The general concept of modified cap weighting is to create diversification in the portfolio. Often the index maker will assign a weight of 1 percent to each security in the portfolio and then adjust up or down from that percentage based on the capitalization. The index weighting does not have to be terribly complicated. Indexes almost always have a maximum cap weight per security. Modifications are usually designed to ensure that no one company or a few companies dominate the index. Sometimes these modifications are related to mutual fund restrictions, which stipulate that the indexes must have diversification. From an index perspective, if it did not meet diversification requirements, no investment manager could hold the weightings. This would render the index useless since a manager or ETF maker could not track the index or use it as a benchmark.

As an index gets more specialized and moves away from broad market exposure, it has to retain acceptable cap-weighting concentrations.

The S&P 500 Sector SPDR ETFs were the first to move away from a broad market index. In these ETFs there was a capping on the large amount of weighting of any one company that could be in the index, and a redistribution of weighting among the other companies in the index. The Nasdaq 100 was another of the indexes that was adjusted to fulfill cap-weighting IRS and SEC requirements, that put limits on how much of an index can be comprised of a single stock and how much of an index can be comprised of the top five stocks. The index was once strictly cap-weighted with its weight dominated by a few companies.

The index in the 1990s was known as the Microsoft index, since it was so heavily weighted by Microsoft. The index has been adjusted so that it is not dominated by any one or a few companies and is now a modified cap-weighted index.

In addition to the IRS issuing rules regarding diversification in indexes, the exchanges have also issued similar requirements. These rules are designed to ensure that an ETF is weighted in a way that allows for diversification.

ACCOMPLISHING WEIGHTING DIVERSIFICATION IN INDEXES

When an indexer is constructing an index that is a candidate to be replicated in performance by an ETF, there is a desire, even in cap-weighted indexes, to construct a reasonably diversified portfolio, while continuing to reflect higher weights for higher capitalized companies. There are different ways to accomplish weighting diversification. For example, an index can be price-weighted, where the dollar price of the securities can have an impact on the portfolio weighting. Or an index can be constructed as a modified cap-weighted index, based on the capitalization value of the stocks. In either modification treatment, there can be caps or floors or breakpoints on the maximum amount of weight for any individual stock or stock groupings.

When an index is constructed, especially if the goal is to have securities offered based on the index, such as an option security, an ETF, or an index-linked note, weighting has to be considered. Even if the index maker has a preference for cap weighting, he or she would want the index to be reasonably diversified, although it could be reflective of higher weighting for the higher-capitalized companies.

NEWER AND UNIQUE ETFS

The Claymore Securities and Van Eck Global ETFs were both released in 2006 and were part of the post-PowerShares wave of ETFs. Both ETF providers have a different approach from each other, and also from other ETFs.

Van Eck Global was founded in 1955, and was among the first U.S. money managers to assist investors in global investing. Today it offers investments in hard assets, emerging markets, precious metals including gold, and other asset classes. Van Eck's offerings are often in asset classes that have low correlation to more traditional U.S. equity and fixed-income investments. Along with offering ETFs and other investments, Van Eck offers a series of variable annuities and variable life policies of highly rated insurers.

Van Eck Global started by launching one security, which is their U.S. Gold Miners ETF (symbol GDX). GDX is a modified cap-weighted ETF, and is comprised of publicly traded companies mostly involved in mining for silver and gold. The ETF contains both common stocks and ADRs.

GDX attempts to replicate the performance, before fees and expenses, of the AMEX Gold Miners Index. It is made up of mostly gold-mining stocks and also includes ADRs of selected companies involved in gold- or silver-ore–mining, and listed on either the AMEX, NYSE, or Nasdaq markets. It attempts to include all stocks that are relevant to the gold sector. As a broad modified cap-weighted index, it is not dominated by one company, but it still retains some of the general relationship of a cap-weighted index. The index is fairly concentrated, containing only 38 stocks, and of these stocks about half are large-cap, about 33 percent are medium-cap, and about 17 percent are small-cap. The index is focused geographically, with about 60 percent of the countries in the index residing in Canada, 16 percent in the United States, and 16 percent in South Africa.

GDX has been developed to fill a niche, making it possible to gain access to a targeted industry group that was not available to the investing public. The ETF is not constructed as an enhanced-selection process or as using an enhanced-weighting scheme, and employs a modified cap-weighted structure.

One of the reasons given for investors to buy gold is gold's low correlation to the stock market. Gold shares often do not go in the same direction of the stock market, and can be a refuge in times of monetary and economic uncertainty. GDX is an efficient way to invest in this sector.

Van Eck Global, as well as some other creators of the new generation of ETFs, is part of a revolution of securities developed to match the needs of investors and traders. Intelligent ETFs include a broad range of securities, including a group of focused niche ETFs, alternatively weighted ETFs, and ETFs using a unique stock selection formula. The Van Eck ETFs are part of the niche group. GDX was well timed in coming to market, and it fits well with the Van Eck corporate expertise. Before it released its ETFs, Van Eck was well known as an active stock manager in precious metals and commodity-related securities. Van Eck understands the precious metals industry very well and ascertained that the AMEX Gold Miners Index was broad enough to be a good benchmark for that industry.

Generally, the fund advisor expects that the ETF will hold the same securities in the same proportions as the Gold Miners Index. However, sometimes it may not be possible or sensible to purchase each security in the exact same weighting. At those times the ETF may buy a sampling of the Gold Miners Index stocks. The advisor may also choose to overweight another security in the index; buy securities for the ETF that are not in the Index as a substitute for other securities; or use combinations of other techniques to replicate, before fees and expenses, the performance of the index.

The ETF may sell securities that it is holding in anticipation of those securities being deleted from the Gold Miners Index or buy securities that it is not holding in anticipation of those securities being added to the Gold Miners Index.

The advisor has the expectation that the correlation between the ETF and the Gold Miners Index, over time and before fees and expenses, will be 95 percent or higher. One hundred percent would be a perfect correlation. Normally the total assets of the ETF will be invested 95 percent in securities that comprise the Gold Miners Index. A lesser percentage may be so invested, depending on the extent that additional flexibility is needed by the advisor to comply with the Internal Revenue Code and other regulatory requirements.

The Gold Miners Index is generally not expected to have frequent or large changes, due to the fact that the fund's portfolio contains many of the characteristics of a long-term investment. Periodically, however, changes could occur as a result of capital changes such as mergers, spin-offs, or a change in the basic business of a company or companies in the index. Portfolio turnover rate is expected to be under 30 percent, because of the passive investment management of the ETF. This is lower than for many other ETFs.

The Gold Miners Index only contains securities of companies with market capitalization greater than $100 million. The daily average traded volume of the companies must be 500,000 shares or greater over the preceding six months.

After offering the U.S. Gold Miners ETF, Van Eck looked for other areas in which to offer ETFs. Van Eck followed up with its Environmental Services ETF (symbol EVX); Steel ETF (symbol SLX); Russia ETF (symbol RSX); Global Alternative Energy, which is also known as a clean energy ETF (symbol GEX).

ENVIRONMENTAL SERVICES ETF

The environment is a big issue, and also a big and growing business. This ETF attempts to replicate, before fees and expenses, the performance of the waste-management companies in the AMEX Environmental Services Index (symbol EVX). The index includes common stocks and ADRs of selected companies that are involved in the management, removal, and storage of consumer waste and industrial by-products, and other environmental services relating to these industries. Currently there are 24 securities in the index, consisting of small-, medium-, and large-cap companies.

The index has performed well. From October 10, 2006 to May 31, 2008, it gained 23.39 percent. This is a hypothetical performance. All performance information prior to September 29, 2006, is hypothetical relying on back-tested data. Performance figures do not include fees and expenses.

The companies eligible for inclusion in the index are those that have a market capitalization of over $100 million. The companies must have a three-month trading price of greater than $3.00, and have a three-month average daily trading volume of over $1 million. Unlike many investment companies, the ETF is not managed on an active basis.

VAN ECK STEEL ETF

It may not be well known that the global steel industry has changed substantially since the early 1900s. Steel production has increased impressively, there has been consolidation in the industry, and recycling has become a widespread practice. Today, as in the past, steel is needed in appliances, cars, furniture, buildings, cans, and virtually every infrastructure item. Steel, in this information technology age, is still an important ingredient needed in every nation's economic growth.

The steel industry is large and complex. Basically there are four segments within the industry: specialty steel companies, integrated steel makers, mini-mills, and service centers. Steel is not of just one type. There are more than 3,000 chemically composed grades of steel, and also steel grades that have specialized requirements. The steel industry is a global enterprise. According to the *New York Times* (June 27, 2006), the steel industry employs 165,000 people, another 1.2 million people indirectly, and contributes $350 billion to the economy. Not only has the steel industry grown, but returns from investing in the companies in the industry have been good. The AMEX constructed the AMEX Steel Index to track companies in this sector. According to studies done by the AMEX, this index would have performed better than the S&P 500 Index from March 30, 2001, through September 30, 2006. These calculations are hypothetical, and are derived from back-tested data for the time periods. Prior to September 29, 2006, the index was not calculated in real time. The AMEX Steel Index is a modified market-cap–weighted index made up of common stocks and ADRs of companies that are primarily involved in activities related to steel production. This includes the operation of mills that manufacture steel, the fabrication of steel products, or the extraction and reduction of iron ore.

Companies selected must be listed on the NYSE, AMEX, or Nasdaq market. The companies must have a market cap of more than $100 million, and have a daily average trading volume of $1 million or more over the last three months. The index weighting is based on the market cap of each of the component securities, modified to conform to two asset diversification requirements, which are applied along with the quarterly adjustments to the index. The first diversification requirement is that the weight of any security may not account for more than 20 percent of the index. The second requirement is that the aggregate weight of those securities that individually represent more than 4.5 percent of the total value of the index may not account for more than 50 percent of the total index value.

The Van Eck Steel ETF (symbol SLX) was launched in October 2006. It is based on its replicating the performance, before fees and expenses, of the AMEX Steel Index. SLX is comprised of 34 securities, including about 78 percent large-cap, about 19 percent medium-cap, and about 2 percent small-cap companies. The geographic breakdown is broad, with about 38 percent of the companies being in North America, about 31 percent in Europe, and 23 percent in South America. The price to earnings ratio appears modest at 16.31 times.

VAN ECK RUSSIA ETF

The Van Eck Russia ETF (symbol RSX) seeks to replicate the performance, before expenses and fees, of the DAXglobal Russia + Index, a modified market-cap–weighted index created to track the movement of selected ADRs and stocks of Russian-domiciled companies that are traded on global exchanges. The index holds about thirty Russian securities.

In 2006 the Russian economy grew over 6 percent, making it an attractive candidate for investors and traders looking to participate in a promising emerging market. Part of the reason for its growth can be attributed to high energy prices and robust consumer spending.

Investors have been attracted to international ETFs, including Russia. RSX is based on an index comprised of securities traded outside of that country, such as on exchanges in New York and London. Russian exchanges do not have a high degree of liquidity, and some lesser active stocks in Russia have a volume of only $10,000 a day.

Russia has growth possibilities, with a high yearly GDP over the last eight years, a high amount of oil and gas revenues, real personal income increasing in double digits, and foreign reserves among the largest in the world. The index has performed well. From April 24, 2007, to May 31, 2008, the index rose 44.21 percent. The performance information is a hypothetical return, and information covering the period before March 26, 2007, is based on back-tested hypothetical data. Prior to March 26, 2007, the index was not calculated in real time, but had a hypothetical back-tested performance. The index invests in about 85 percent large-cap securities, about 6 percent mid-cap, and about 8 percent small-cap securities. The sectors invested in include the following approximate industry percentages: oil and gas, about 39 percent; iron and steel, 19 percent; telecommunications, 17 percent; electric, 10 percent; and finance, 8 percent.

Russia's main industries include oil and gas exploration and production, steel production, the generation of electricity, and mining.

For entry into the index, only companies that have a market cap larger than $150 million with a daily average trading volume of $1 million or more over the last six months are eligible. The index weighting is based on the market cap of each of the component securities, modified to conform to its asset diversification requirements, which are applied in coordination with the index quarterly adjustments. The index is reviewed quarterly to ensure that the securities that make up the index represent the Russian company universe. At its choosing, Van Eck may replace securities in the index with others if, in its judgment, such addition, deletion, or substitution is necessary or appropriate to maintain the quality and integrity of the index.

The portfolio turnover rate is expected to be under 30 percent, which is a low turnover rate compared to other indexes.

GLOBAL ALTERNATIVE ENERGY ETF

Global Alternative Energy ETF (symbol GEX) was developed to offer investors and traders exposure to the alternative energy industry. GEX is also known as a clean air ETF. This ETF's objective is to replicate, before fees and expenses, the performance of the Ardour Global Index (Extra Liquid). The index is a rules-based index to give investors and traders exposure to the overall performance of a global universe of listed companies that are engaged in the alternative energy industry.

The Ardour Global Index is a modified cap-weighted, float-adjusted index comprised of publicly traded companies involved in the production of alternative fuels and/or technologies that are engaged in the production of alternative energy power (the AGI industry). The index attempts to include all the global companies principally engaged in alternative energy. The index is comprised of the 30 stocks in the AGI Composite Index that have the highest average of daily trading volume and the highest market capitalization.

Stocks must have a market cap of over $100 million on a set index rebalancing date. Any stock whose market cap has dropped below $50 million as of any rebalancing reconstitution date will be deleted from the index. To be included in the AGI Composite Index, stocks must have a three-month average daily trading price of $1.00 or more per share.

The index is rather evenly split, with about 38 percent comprised of large-cap stocks, about 38 percent in mid-cap, and about 22 percent in small-cap issues. About 41 percent of the companies in the index are domiciled in the United States, 17 percent in Germany, and the rest scattered about the globe. The price to earnings ratio is a rich 48.53 times.

VAN ECK WEIGHTING METHODOLOGY

The Van Eck ETFs are based on offering exposure to target industry groups, and less on a weighting or weighting to stock selection method. For instance, with SLX Van Eck is offering exposure to publicly traded domestic and foreign companies involved in producing steel products or mining and processing of iron ore.

In the Environmental Services ETF (symbol EVX), Van Eck is offering exposure to the increasing issues of cleaning up. Whether water cleanup, waste management, or pollution issues, the ETF offers exposure to the companies that are poised to benefit from this activity. Van Eck attempts to be the first to offer exposure in the areas it covers. The clean energy exposure offered through GEX allows traders and investors to track the global performance of listed companies operating in the alternative energy industry.

The Russian ETF (symbol RSX) was offered by Van Eck because it saw Russia as a key emerging market. Van Eck identified an area that it thought was important exposure for investors and traders, and constructed an ETF to attempt to replicate the performance of that index. Nevertheless, RSX was not the first Russian ETF, and GEX, the Global Alternative Energy ETF, was not the first to offer exposure to that country.

There is an alternative-weighting component to Van Eck's ETFs. Most focused niche products tend to need some sort of modified equal-weight or modified-cap–weighted index construction for an ETF to be fairly diversified for regulatory reasons and also to be useful to traders and investors.

In constructing the Russian ETF, Van Eck used an approach that is common in other ETFs, which is that it used ADRs and GDRs rather than buying stocks in the home market of the stock issuers. GDRs are Global Depository Receipts, certificates issued by a depository bank such as JPMorgan Chase or Deutsche Bank. The certificates represent ownership of shares and are traded and settled independently of the underlying shares, and are usually used to trade in companies in emerging markets, especially Russia. GDRs trade on the London Stock Exchange.

Chapter | 9

CLAYMORE SECURITIES

Claymore entered the ETF market by offering its shares in 2006, and it has been aggressive in creating new ETFs by offering 29 new securities. Claymore does not have one central concept that anchors all of its securities; instead, it has brought out several securities with many index providers all focused on adding value through the various index constructions.

Claymore has a long history of offering financial securities, including unit investment trusts, closed-end funds, and mutual funds. Claymore is constantly searching for new securities to bring into the market and has been innovative in its offerings.

For instance, one of the first ETFs Claymore offered was the Claymore/Zacks Yield Hog ETF, which focuses on an investor's concern for diversified yield.

CLAYMORE/ZACKS YIELD HOG ETF
Claymore/Zacks Yield Hog ETF (symbol CVY) attempts to replicate, before fees and expenses, the performance of the Zacks Yield Hog Index. Rather than buy the same securities as the index, CVY uses a

sampling approach in replicating the performance. Sampling means that Claymore will quantitatively select securities from the index universe to create a representative portfolio that resembles the index in factors such as risk characteristics, and will attempt to match the approximate performance of the index. The companies are selected by a proprietary methodology developed by Zacks, which is designed to choose companies with high income potential and superior risk-reward profiles.

Each company within each investment type is ranked using a quantitative rules-based method. The types of factors considered are yield, a company's growth record, stock liquidity, and relative values. Companies are sorted by the Zacks methodology and are ranked from the highest to the lowest in terms of desirability. If practicable, CVY can replicate the securities exactly to match its performance goals. The portfolio is reconstituted and rebalanced quarterly.

Normally, CVY will invest at least 90 percent of its assets into the securities that make up the index. The index is comprised of about 125 to 150 securities selected from a universe of global securities, based on investment merit and other criteria.

In addition to U.S. listed common stocks, CVY can invest in dividend-paying ADRs, Real Estate Investment Trusts, Master Limited Partnerships, closed-end funds, and preferred stocks. Fifty percent or more of the portfolio will consist of dividend-paying common stocks. Closed-end funds are limited to 10 percent of the portfolio, and Master Limited Partnerships may not make up more than 25 percent of the portfolio. ADRs, REITs, preferreds, and other investment types, other than U.S. common stocks, are limited to 20 percent per investment type.

CLAYMORE/SABRIENT STEALTH ETF

The Claymore/Sabrient Stealth ETF (symbol STH) is classified as a small-cap blend type, meaning it encompasses both growth and value in the small-cap stock universe. Basically, the ETF seeks neglected stocks to put into its portfolio.

STH attempts to replicate the performance, before fees and expenses, of the Sabrient Stealth Index. Normally, STH will invest 90 percent or more of its assets in the securities that comprise the index. Claymore seeks a correlation of 95 percent or better, over time, between the performance of STH and the index.

Since Sabrient began publishing its rankings in April 2002, its stock selections have shown good performance. They have consistently outperformed their relevant benchmarks over a broad range of investing styles, market cap sizes, time frames, and market conditions.

Sabrient provides fundamentals-based quantitative equity research that is analyst bias free and is customized to each client's investing strategy or style. Among other customized quantitative modeling, it performs index rankings of many of the common market indexes, from S&P to Russell, with details from its top-performing filters.

STH employs a passive approach to replicating the index performance. This index is comprised of approximately 150 securities that are selected, based on investment and other criteria, from a broad universe of U.S. listed stocks and ADRs that have little or no Wall Street analyst coverage. Little or no coverage means that there are not more than two analysts covering the considered securities.

The Stealth Index selection methodology is designed to identify companies with potentially superior risk-return profiles as determined by Sabrient. The index objective is to offer exposure to a group of stocks that are flying under the radar of Wall Street's analysts, but which have displayed growth characteristics that give them the potential to outperform, on a risk-adjusted basis, the Russell 2000 Small Cap Index and other small-cap–oriented benchmark indexes.

Sabrient developed the index constituent selection methodology, which is a quantitative approach to selecting stocks in a diversified portfolio. The index member selection process selects stocks from a universe of uncovered and undercovered companies using its own proprietary, 100 percent rules-based methodology. The index constituent selection methodology uses its multifactor proprietary selection rules to select those stocks that offer the greatest potential from a risk-return perspective while maintaining industry diversification. The approach is designed to enhance investment applications and investability. The index is adjusted quarterly.

CLAYMORE/SABRIENT INSIDER

The Claymore/Sabrient Insider ETF (symbol NFO) is classified as mid-cap growth, which means that it is comprised of stocks that are medium-sized and have outstanding growth characteristics. The ETF is seeking stocks that have strong buying sentiment from company insiders.

NFO seeks to replicate the investment results, before fees and expenses, of the Sabrient Insider Sentiment Index. The fund normally will invest at least 90 percent of its assets in common stocks and ADRs that comprise the index. Claymore Advisors seeks a correlation over time of 95 percent or better between the performance of NFO and the index performance. NFO uses a low-cost passive-investment approach in seeking to replicate the performance of the index. The index is comprised of approximately 100 stocks that are selected on their investment merit and other criteria from a broad universe of U.S. listed stocks and ADRs.

The Insider Sentiment Index selection methodology seeks to identify companies with potentially superior risk-return profiles as determined by Sabrient Systems LLC. The index attempts to give exposure to securities that reflect favorable corporate insider buying trends that are determined by the public filings of corporate insiders. Also considered are earnings increases as reported by Wall Street analysts. This gives companies that are placed in the index the potential to outperform the S&P 500 Index and other broad market benchmark indexes on a risk-adjusted basis.

Sabrient evaluates corporate insider buying trends and earnings estimate increases by Wall Street analysts in its ranking process when considering companies for possible index inclusion. It is possible for a company that scores high enough on either one of those factors to be included in the index based on one factor alone.

The index selection methodology uses multifactor proprietary selection rules to identify those stocks that are believed to offer the greatest potential from a risk-return perspective while maintaining industry diversification. The approach is designed to enhance investment applications and investability. The index is adjusted quarterly to ensure timely stock selections.

All equities that trade on the major U.S. exchanges are considered. Every company is ranked using a quantitative rules-based methodology that includes composite scoring of a handful of specially targeted factors and is sorted from highest to lowest, according to a securities selection methodology developed by Sabrient. The 100 highest-ranking stocks are chosen and given an equal weighting in the portfolio.

The Constituent Selection Process and portfolio rebalance is repeated once per quarter.

CLAYMORE/ROBECO DEVELOPED INTERNATIONAL EQUITY ETF

The Claymore/Robeco Developed International Equity ETF (symbol EEN) is classified as a world stock portfolio. It is comprised of stocks that attempt to give exposure to attractive companies in the developed world. The Claymore/Robeco Developed International Equity ETF seeks investment results that correspond generally to the performance, before fees and expenses, of the Robeco Developed International Equity Index.

The fund will normally invest at least 90 percent of its total assets in equities that comprise the index and in ADRs based on the securities in the index. Claymore Advisors seeks a correlation over time of 95 percent or better between the EEN performance and the performance of the index. EEN uses a low-cost passive investment approach. The index is comprised of, at any given time, between 100 and 200 stocks. These stocks are selected based on their liquidity, ease of trading, valuation and momentum measures, and other criteria.

The index tracks the performance of liquid, tradable global equities. The universe includes all equities listed on international developed market exchanges. Aggregate country weightings are based on the aggregate market capitalization of each country's constituents, modified to account for liquidity and risk. The weighting methodology is designed to achieve broad-based global diversification while enhancing tradability.

Potential candidates for the index include globally listed equities that meet minimum liquidity, tradability, and other requirements, with market capitalizations of approximately U.S. $1 billion or greater. Stocks considered for the index are selected using a rules-driven quantitative methodology proprietary to Robeco. The index seeks to establish a representation of each developed country's aggregate modified market capitalization. Each stock is ranked using a proprietary multifactor stock selection model and sorted from most attractive to least attractive. The model identifies attractive stocks based on valuation factors such as book value-to-price ratio; momentum factors, such as price return over the past 6 to 12 months; earnings revision factors, which consider positive and negative revisions to consensus earnings estimates; and management policy factors, such as share buybacks.

The constituent selection methodology was developed by Robeco as a quantitative, rules-driven approach to identifying those companies that offer the greatest potential for price appreciation with strong risk diversification. Portfolio risk-management tools, including a quantitative risk model and portfolio optimizer, are used to balance risk and reward. The amount of each country's allocation is based on its aggregate modified market capitalization. Stock rebalancing is done monthly, and universe reconstitution is completed annually.

THE VARIED CLAYMORE ETF APPROACH

Claymore has taken different approaches to develop niche ETFs needed by investors and traders. The one consistent factor that Claymore has sustained across the range of its ETF offerings is that, within each of these categories, Claymore has looked for index providers who were offering an approach that added value. This fits well with the overall theme of considering intelligent ETFs in a broad context, stating that there is no one way to analyze whether an ETF is intelligent—each ETF must be judged on its own.

ETF providers do not have to offer just one style or type of ETFs. PowerShares, for example, offers its Intellidex group of ETFs that employ a quantitative method to seek alpha. It also offers alternative-weighted ETFs, as well as niche-sector specialized ETFs. All PowerShares offerings are intelligent, although constructed differently from one another. PowerShares and the other intelligent ETF makers are designing their ETFs to accomplish varied goals, and the goals are not specific to any one sector, geographic region, or any other single investment niche.

Claymore has offered value-added-style ETFs and also ETFs that give exposure to key regions, such as their BRIC ETF. This ETF offers investment exposure to Brazil, Russia, India, and China, some of the fastest-growing countries in the world.

CLAYMORE BRIC ETF

Claymore BRIC ETF (symbol EEB) is constructed to allow investors and traders exposure to companies located in the BRIC countries: Brazil, Russia, India, and China. Claymore and many other investment professionals think there is growth potential in these emerging countries. Reports show that the combined average annual GDP growth of these countries has been higher than other leading countries over the last 10 years.

An investment of $10,000 in the BNY BRIC Index over the period of December 31, 2001, to December 31, 2006, would have returned

$42,087, compared with a return of $33,006 if placed into the MSCI EM Index (Source: BNY BRIC Select ADR Index and Bloomberg). The BNY BRIC Select ADR Index performances are hypothetical. The performance data for both indexes assumes the reinvestment of dividends.

EEB attempts to replicate, net of expenses, the performance of the BNY BRIC Select ADR Index. This index tracks the performance of companies from the BRIC countries, which trade as ADRs or GDRs on a U.S. stock exchange. The index uses ADRs or GDRs for exposure for the BRIC country equities because the stock markets in those countries are rather underdeveloped and do not offer enough liquidity or high enough listing standards.

Companies selected for inclusion into the index have to meet the following criteria. The ADRs or GDRs must be listed on one of three U.S. exchanges: the NYSE, the AMEX, or the Nasdaq. The price of the ADR or GDR has to be $3.00 or more. The minimum three-month average trading volume of the ADR has to be 25,000 shares or greater, or 125,000 shares of stock. Free float-adjusted market capitalization has to be $250 million or greater.

The country security breakdown as of May 2008, is Brazil, 53.56 percent; China, 32.24 percent; India, 8.84 percent; and Russia, 5.31 percent. The sector breakdown is highly concentrated with four sectors making up most of the index: Energy, 26.16 percent; Telecommunication Services, 20.02 percent; Financials, 15.70 percent; and Materials, 20.89 percent.

Some analysts think that BRIC countries should grow at a higher annual rate over the next 10 years than developed nations such as the United States, United Kingdom, and France. There are risks investing in emerging markets, to which EEB offers exposure. However, the potential of the EEB countries is compelling. Jim O'Neill, global economist at Goldman Sachs, opines that the economic potential of the BRIC countries is such that they could become among the four most dominant countries by the year 2050.

CLAYMORE S&P GLOBAL WATER INDEX ETF

Among the first ETFs offered by Claymore was a global water ETF, the Claymore S&P Global Water Index ETF (symbol CGW). CGW attempts to replicate the S&P Global Water Index and is the first U.S. listed global water ETF. The index tracks companies that are involved in water-related businesses in developed countries around the globe. The index is comprised of 50 stocks.

There are two types of companies in the water industry that are placed in the index. The first is the water utilities and infrastructure companies and the second is the water equipment and material companies. The index is evenly split between the two types, with 25 companies in each.

Water utilities and infrastructure companies are those engaged in activities such as water supply, water utilities, wastewater treatment, and sewer and pipeline construction. Water and equipment companies include, among their activities, water-treatment chemicals, water-treatment appliance pumps, and pumping equipment.

CGW is comprised of small-, medium-, and large-cap stocks. Both common stocks and ADRs are placed in the index. Country weighting is heavily concentrated with about 78 percent of the index companies domiciled in the United States, France, Japan, and the United Kingdom.

The index methodology that decides which companies will be placed in the index includes how much weight the relative importance of the global water industry is in the overall company business structure.

THE CLAYMORE OIL SANDS SECTOR ETF

This ETF is created to offer traders and investors exposure to companies focused on oil sands production. The Claymore Oil Sands Sector ETF (symbol CLO) trades on the Toronto Stock Exchange and seeks to replicate the performance, before fees and expenses, of the Sustainable Oil Sands Sector Index. The ETF is traded in two classes of securities: a common unit and an advisor class unit.

According to Claymore, this is one of the fastest-growing industries in the energy sector of Canada, and Canadian oil sands are among the largest oil reserves in the world. The index is focused on companies that are involved in producing oil sands, and which are expected to increase their oil sands production over the next 10 years.

The index weighting is based on a mathematical formula that considers five factors of a company's operation. By concentrating on these factors, the index creators think the index will invest in the companies that best represent the present and future oil sands production. The five company factors are (1) production as measured by barrels of oil sands per day; (2) projected production of oil sands as measured by barrels per day; (3) percentage of the company's total percentage of total production focused on oil sands production; (4) the company's market liquidity; and (5) the company's market capitalization.

Claymore thinks that CLO is attractive because the long-term prospects for oil demand is promising, and the companies in the ETF will benefit from this growth. Strong and increasing demand from robust economies in places like China and India will continue, putting stress on the oil demand-supply equation. This could keep oil prices high. There are huge reserves of Canadian oil sands, which could grow more valuable in the future.

CLO is focused and includes only 15 companies. The average price to earnings ratio is about 15 times.

According to data supplied by Claymore Securities (Source: Sustainable Oil Sands Sector Index and Bloomberg; as of 12/31/06; figures annualized), the index performed well. Over a two-year period the index returned 55.55 percent, versus 31.66 percent for the S&P/TSX Capped Energy Index. The index returns are hypothetical, and do not take into account fees and other expenses.

THE CLAYMORE/OCEAN TOMO PATENT ETF

Claymore, among its other associations, has a relationship with the financial structure firm Ocean Tomo, LLC.

Ocean Tomo is a leading merchant banking firm, specializing in understanding and leveraging intellectual property assets. The company is engaged in activities such as advising on mergers and acquisitions, conducting valuations, and performing intellectual property auctions.

The Claymore/Ocean Tomo Patent ETF (symbol OTP) attempts to replicate, before fees and expenses, the performance of the Ocean Tomo 300 Patent Index, which is the first publicly traded patent index. About 300 companies comprise the index. The index is designed to reflect six companies within 50 style and size groups, including value, relative value, blend, growth at a reasonable price (GARP), and growth by decile. The companies are selected with the highest value-to-book ratio as chosen by Ocean Tomo, LLC.

The index seeks to represent a grouping of companies that own quality patent portfolios. One thousand companies are evaluated for the index. The methodology for the companies comprising the index was developed by Ocean Tomo.

CLAYMORE/ZACKS SECTOR ROTATION ETF

Claymore/Zacks Sector Rotation ETF (symbol XRO) seeks to replicate the performance, before fees and expenses, of the Zacks Sector Rotation Index. XRO will normally invest at least 90 percent of its total assets in common stocks and ADRs that comprise the index. The ETF seeks a correlation over time of 95 percent or better between its performance and the index's performance. XRO uses a passive approach in attempting to replicate the performance of the index. The Zacks Sector Rotation Index is comprised of 100 stocks that are selected from a universe of the 1,000 largest listed equity companies based on market capitalization.

The Zacks Sector Rotation Index uses a proprietary quantitative methodology developed by Zacks to over weight sectors with potentially superior risk-return profiles. The objective of the index is to over weight those sectors that combined have the potential to outperform on a risk-adjusted basis the S&P 500 Index and other benchmark indexes. The methodology for selecting securities uses proprietary selection rules to identify sectors that offer the greatest potential from a risk-return perspective. The approach is designed to enhance investment applications and investability.

All U.S. equities and U.S. exchange-listed ADRs that rank as the 1,000 largest based on market capitalization are considered for inclusion in the index. The index strives to over weight cyclical sectors prior to anticipated periods of economic expansion and over weight noncyclical sectors prior to anticipated periods of economic contraction. Sector allocations are chosen based on a Zacks proprietary quantitative methodology using the 16 Zacks Expanded Sectors. These sectors consist of Consumer Staples, Consumer Discretionary, Retail-Wholesale, Medical, Auto-Tires-Trucks, Basic Materials, Industrial Products, Construction, Multi-Sector Conglomerates, Computer-Technology, Aerospace, Oils/Energy, Finance, Utilities, Transportation, and Business Services.

The index uses a bottom-up approach to decide on the weightings of each sector based on relative value, insider trading, price momentum, earnings growth, earnings estimate revision, and earnings surprise, as well as quantitative macroeconomic factors that focus on the business cycle.

Exposure for any one sector may range from no exposure to a maximum of 45 percent of the index. Stocks are selected based on liquidity. Individual stock exposure will be determined by relative market capitalization within the sector. No individual stock may consist of more than 5 percent of the total index.

The sector allocation and constituent ranking, reconstitution, and rebalancing process are done quarterly.

CLAYMORE ETF HISTORY

The ETFs described in the section above were among the first brought out by Claymore. All fit into the key area of interest as indicated by traders and investors. Claymore continues to create ETFs that are useful and needed and delivers these to the investing public. It does not tie itself in with any one index provider or any one solution.

The Claymore BRIC ETF (symbol EEB) was offered in September 2006 along with Claymore/Zacks Yield Hog (symbol CVY), Claymore/Sabrient Insider (symbol NFO), and Claymore/Sabrient Stealth ETF (symbol STH). Also at this time Claymore offered the Claymore/Zacks Sector Rotation ETF (symbol XRO).

Claymore Securities has been involved in many different types of research endeavors but always with the same core concept of delivering creative key investment performances as investment characteristics.

Chapter | 10

SPECIALIZED ETF APPROACHES

FIRST TRUST PORTFOLIOS

Many ETF makers were significant financial institutions before they started developing and launching ETFs. Among others, Claymore and Van Eck had long-term experience in their mutual fund operations and other asset-management activities.

First Trust Portfolios was experienced also. It had a major closed-end fund and was among the largest marketers of unit investment trusts (UITs) well before it became an ETF maker. When intelligent ETFs were launched, First Trust announced it would be offering its first ETF, based on replicating a Dow Jones micro-cap index.

The barriers of entry for first-time ETF makers are higher than barriers for makers that already have ETFs on the market. Because of these barriers, it takes a while to get set up and get mechanisms in place for first-time ETF offerings.

By the time First Trust launched its first ETF—the First Trust Dow-Jones Select Micro-Cap ETF (symbol FDM)—BGI and PowerShares already had a micro-cap ETF trading in the market. So First Trust's ETF was the third of its type in the market, although they were the first maker to publicly file for this ETF type.

FIRST TRUST PORTFOLIOS' ETFs

Among its ETF offerings, First Trust offered the First Trust Amex Biotechnology Index Fund (symbol FBT), which is based on an index created by the American Stock Exchange. This index was created some time ago, and originally was designed to be an equal-weighted options index.

First Trust also offers a Dow Jones Internet Index Fund (symbol FDN) and an IPO-related ETF, the IPOX–100 Index Fund (symbol FPX).

The Morningstar Dividend Leader Index Fund (symbol FDL) includes stocks from one of the three major exchanges: NYSE, AMEX, or Nasdaq. The stocks chosen for inclusion in the ETF are those that have shown dividend consistency and sustainability. Real Estate Investment Trusts (REITs) are excluded.

Morningstar's proprietary multistep screening process is used to select a universe of stocks. The top 100 stocks, based on dividend yield, are selected for the index. The individual holdings are weighted based on each security's shares outstanding, free-float factor, and annual indicated dividend per share. To enhance diversification, the weighting of each holding is capped.

These are varied ETFs. They were launched because First Trust felt they were opportunistic, and in market segments that First Trust thought should be covered.

ALPHADEX ENHANCED INDEX ETF SERIES

Some really interesting ETFs that First Trust launched in 2007 were its AlphaDEX Enhanced Index series, which is a new ETF family. This series includes both sector and style ETFs, using a very simple algorithm to make an enhanced index.

Different index types were used. First Trust used indexes from S&P, from the AMEX, and from Dow Jones. For their enhancement methodology across its index types, First Trust looks at factors that allow it to determine which stocks to eliminate from its stock screened universe, basing elimination on those stocks least likely to perform.

Whereas most other stock selection and weighting methods focus on finding stocks to include in a portfolio, this method whittles down the numbers of constituent stocks, with the goal of dropping the lower-performing ones. Using this method the portfolio ends up including about 75 percent of the analyzed stock universe. The portfolio is weighted using a modified weighting method.

Selecting stocks and weighting this way is interesting in that, instead of searching for stocks to add alpha, the index is searching for stocks that will drag down performance and then it eliminates those stocks. This is a powerful concept from a portfolio management perspective.

There is a great benefit to using this method for stock picking for an index. This method cuts down on the drag on performance that occurs as a consequence of poorly performing stocks. In this way the indexes end up with a broad market exposure. With this method the market is set up into quartiles. The index holds the top three quartiles and drops the bottom quartiles, based on the index ranking system.

The AlphaDEX indexes end up with broad market coverage. The companies end up slightly differently weighted based on how the company has scored. This is an interesting approach, and one that has applied well throughout a period of time. As a screening method for index calculations, it was not uncommon, especially in the 1990s, to structure a note or UIT from this sort of screen. This screen chooses stocks for consideration, and the portfolio managers take the best stocks from the screen and drop every other stock from the portfolio.

Enhanced indexing usually seeks to identify stocks from a broad-based index—stocks that exhibit characteristics that will provide the greatest potential for capital appreciation. Enhanced indexing seeks to generate positive alpha relative to the broad-based index from which it selects its stocks. Enhanced indexing is itself passive. No active judgment is used in evaluating stocks, and the process is driven by a transparent, repeatable quantitative process.

The AlphaDEX process uses custom enhanced indexes created and administered by S&P and/or the AMEX. These indexes then employ the proprietary rules-based AlphaDEX stock selection methodology.

WAYS TO WEIGHT AND ADD INTELLIGENCE TO INDEXING

Index makers use methods that are focused on selecting stocks for index inclusion and enhancement. Some indexing methods are also focused on weighting stocks in the portfolio. Some strategies combine these two methods. ETFs are then created to replicate the performance of those indexes.

For example, PowerShares offers ETFs that attempt to replicate the performance of indexes based on the Intellidex method of stock screening. This selection is based on quantitative models—models that select a small number of stocks from a large stock universe. PowerShares also offers the Research Affiliates Fundamental Indexation (RAFI) family of ETFs. This family focuses on reweighting stock from a large stock universe.

The AlphaDEX series focuses on culling the worst stocks from a large stock universe. Also there is a reweighting from the large stock universe when the stock universe has been selected.

Index makers can take many approaches. Since enhanced indexing can proceed in so many different ways, there is a vast variety of ETFs to choose from to accomplish your investing or trading goals. For example, an ETF maker can concentrate in a narrow sector or group, increasing the risk of holding an ETF that has little diversification, but giving the profit potential that this type of ETF offers.

HEALTHSHARES

A good example of a particularly targeted approach is HealthShares, a newer ETF maker. HealthShares ETFs are targeted on specific therapies. HealthShares claims that most index creation is horizontal, with managers picking the best-known companies. It believes that the best opportunities in the health-care field can only be found by digging beneath the surface to get to know the companies very well that go into the index. It refers to this as *vertical index creation.*

The HealthShares family is composed of 20 ETFs that seek to replicate the performances of its indexes. The HealthShares Composite ETF holds 80 stocks. The other ETFs, which can be found on their Web site, hold 22 to 25 stocks.

Their ETFs are constructed to provide diversification as well as concentrated exposure to a vertical strategy. The ETFs are organized by therapeutic categories in pharmaceuticals, health-care services, life sciences, and biotechnology. Each ETF seeks investment results that correspond to the performance, before fees and expenses, of an equity index of publicly traded common stocks and ADRs. The companies in the portfolios are selected using a proprietary method developed by XShares Group, LLC and are designed to identify companies in the specific health-care vertical or subsector.

The ETFs employ a passive management investment approach designed to track the performance of its underlying index. Funds will generally invest at least 90 percent of its assets in common stocks of companies in the underlying index.

ETF APPROACHES IN THE INFORMATION TECHNOLOGY GROUP

The information technology (IT) sector has often led market advances in the past, and a good IT sector earnings performance could help bolster stock market performance. Still, investors remember that the stock market had a bear market down leg starting in 2000, and much of the loss was in the IT sector. Earnings were sharply down in this sector then. Should investors continue to be concerned about profitability in the high-tech sector?

Many argue it would be hard to see strong markets without participation of the IT sector. As far as the U.S. economy, and to an extent the worldwide economy, we have seen in this book that technology has to be a leader for stability and growth. Technology is a driver that has been important for the economy and the stock market for some time, increasingly so over the last 20 years.

"WAS THERE TOO LITTLE ENTRY DURING THE DOT-COM ERA?": THE STUDY

IT could be in the early stage of development, especially in the Internet consumer area, and poised to continue its worldwide expansion with good earnings growth. An April 2006 study by Goldfarb and Kirsch (University of Maryland) and Miller (University of California, San Diego), titled "Was There Too Little Entry During the Dot-Com Era?" (Working Paper No. RHS–06–029) pointed out that between March 2000 and September 2002, the stock market decline resulted in a $4.4 trillion loss of company value.

Much of the stock market loss was caused by the collapse of dot-com industry companies. Yet, each $1 invested by venture capitalists (VCs) into a portfolio of dot-com companies in 1995 to 2000 was still worth $1.80 at the end of 2001. So the VCs made money, which would suggest that most of the money lost in the IT collapse was lost by those people who bought and traded the IT IPOs in the secondary market, after the IT companies had gone public.

Another surprising conclusion of the report is that instead of too many companies going into the dot-com business, too few went in.

A TOO-SMALL INTERNET INDUSTRY

The reason for too few companies entering the IT market was because the VCs believed in their broadly held but erroneous theory that to make it in that industry, companies had to "Get Big Fast" (GBF). The VCs believed that the companies that would be successful had to map out a niche by attracting "eyeballs" and grow quickly, so that competition could not enter their niche.

The companies that wanted to enter a market found it difficult or impossible to enter since VCs, who were interested only in creating giants that would fit their GBF theory, would not supply the needed capital to enter.

GBF proved to be a faulty premise. Many smaller companies have created a presence and made money on the Internet. Many of the newer companies are not giants, but are profitable companies that have tens to hundreds of millions of dollars in sales.

Another reason that VCs believed in the GBF theory was that it matched their investment objectives. The study points out that "VCs and entrepreneurs may have different success criteria: a lifestyle business might be successful in the eyes of the entrepreneur, but would not be a successful investment for a VC." Goldfarb, Kirsch, and Miller made clear that a VC might invest in an Internet business, and if the business is viable as a lifestyle business but unlikely to prove a substantial cash-out opportunity, the VC might shut the business down for its salvage value. A non-VC–backed firm might continue operations. Hence, whereas the performance of both firms is similar, the survival outcome would be different.

If an entrepreneur could make a successful business out of an Internet company, enough to support his lifestyle, but the company would not be successful enough for a VC to make the money needed for her investment, then perhaps the figures regarding the Internet industry are misleading.

This study concludes that "the survival rate of Dot-Com firms was on a par with or higher than other emerging industries" (Goldfarb, Kirsch, Miller, p. 3). This conclusion flies in the face of the conventional wisdom that the industry collapsed. Conventional wisdom suggests that too many IT companies, especially Internet companies, came to market; the market couldn't handle it; and this is why many failed.

Although the stock market experienced an Internet sector collapse in the market down leg starting in 2000, IT is still an emerging industry. There are niches to expand into, room for companies to grow, and the industry is still early in its growth. The future of the Internet, and the concomitant IT industry, is bright and getting brighter, and this sector could very well continue to lead market advances.

LOOKING FORWARD TO THE FUTURE OF THE TECH SECTOR

The operating earnings for the IT sector appear good for the year 2008. Estimates, as usual, are subject to uncertainties of the U.S. and global economies. Chief among these are the depths of the subprime problems, the housing problems, global deal making, and currency fluctuations.

Standard and Poor's estimates that the IT sector will gain about 17 percent in the year 2008 versus the year 2007, resulting in a PE of around 18. For the year 2009 the estimate calls for an increase of 22.5 percent, resulting in a PE for the sector of 15.5.

Also the Telcom sector is estimated by Standard and Poor's to have good earnings in 2008. The sector should have about 24 percent increase over 2007. If these earnings come to fruition, the sector will have reasonable multiples by historical standards. In fact, Standard and Poor's estimates that the multiple on its S&P 500 Index in 2008 will be about 15.83 times. This is another reasonable multiple by historical standards. For instance, in the quarter ended March 31,

2002, the S&P 500 Index was 46.45 times. This was an anomaly, but should be taken into account when considering the 2008 estimated multiple.

ETF REPRESENTATION IN THE TECH SECTOR

There are many ETFs that offer representation to this sector. Also, there are ETFs that offer broad market representation and have an IT tilt. Following are some ETFs to consider.

NYSE ARCA TECH 100 ETF

Ziegler Capital Management is an investment-management services company that brought out the NYSE Arca Tech 100 ETF (symbol NXT) in March 2007. The index that NXT attempts to replicate, before fees and expenses, is the NYSE Arca Tech 100 Index, launched in 1982. The former ArcaEx was the first open, electronic stock exchange in the United States. The NYSE took over Arca and the name was changed to NYSE Arca. The company has a leading position in trading ETFs and exchange listed securities. Equity options are also traded on the NYSE Arca.

This index was being used as a benchmark by Ziegler Capital for a traditional fund that Ziegler offered.

NXT seeks to offer investors and traders exposure to an index that has a long-term performance record and a diversified portfolio relating to technology. NYSE Arca Tech 100 Index consists of 100 companies from a variety of technology-related industries. The index is constructed to offer a multi-industry technology exposure, with the index measuring the performance of technology-driven companies that are involved in innovations in their industry.

NXT offers a diversified approach to investing in various technology disciplines and also traditional sectors such as media, aerospace, biotechnology, and various computer sectors such as hardware and software. Companies from various industries that develop or use innovative technology in their business are considered for the index.

The industry breakdown represented in the index is diverse. Software is 17.91 percent; Semiconductors, 14.44 percent; Telecommunications, 11.75 percent; and the balance scattered over 15 other subsectors. The index is price-weighted, meaning that the stocks are not weighted by market capitalization but by the dollar price of the shares. This weighting can give more weight to smaller capitalized companies.

The index has performed well. According to NYSE Arca, the index has outperformed the Nasdaq 100 Index, the Dow Jones U.S. Technology Sector Index, and the S&P Tech Select Sector Index over the 3-, 5-, and 10-year periods ending June 30, 2007. From its inception in 1982, the index has returned a 14.11 percent average yearly return.

NASDAQ 100 EQUAL-WEIGHTED ETF

The objective of the Nasdaq 100 Equal-Weighted ETF (symbol QQEW) is to replicate as closely as possible, before fees and expenses, the price and yield of the Nasdaq 100 Equal-Weighted Index.

QQEW consists of companies in the Nasdaq 100 Index. Stocks in the ETF are reconstituted once a year in December, but replacements may be made during the year if a replacement is made in the index. The index is equal-weighted, and is rebalanced four times a year. QQEW contains the same securities as the Nasdaq 100 Index. Each of the securities is initially set at a weight of 1.00 percent of the index and is rebalanced quarterly. The Nasdaq 100 Index includes 100 of the largest nonfinancial securities listed on the Nasdaq Stock Exchange. The equal weighting structure allows for the performance of the small and mid-sized companies to contribute as much as the large companies within the index.

NASDAQ 100 TECHNOLOGY SECTOR INDEX ETF

The investment objective of Nasdaq 100 Technology Sector Index ETF (symbol QTEF) is to replicate as closely as possible, before fees and expenses, the price and yield of the Nasdaq 100 Technology Sector Index.

The index consists of companies in the Nasdaq 100 Index classified as Technology according to the Industry Classification Benchmark (ICB). QTEF is reconstituted once a year based on the Nasdaq 100 Index reconstitution in December, but replacements may be made during the year if there is a replacement in the index. QTEF is equal weighted, and is rebalanced four times a year.

NASDAQ 100 ETF

PowerShares is the sponsor of one of the most actively traded equity securities in the world, the PowerShares QQQ (symbol QQQQ). QQQQ seeks to replicate the Nasdaq 100 Index, which includes the 100 largest nonfinancial companies that trade on the Nasdaq Stock Exchange. QQQQ opened for trading in March 1999 and set a first-day trading record, with 2.6 million shares being traded.

Inclusion in this index is mostly according to the market size of the company. Besides size, companies that go in the index have to have some seasoning. The company has to have been traded on the Nasdaq or other recognized exchange for about two years. Nasdaq does not want to put a company in the index that has just gone public, even if it does meet the size criterion.

The company has to be a nonfinancial index because Nasdaq has a separate index for financials, which is the Nasdaq Financial 100 Index. Unlike other major indexes, such as the S&P 500 Index, non-U.S. companies are included in the index. Stocks put in the index must have had an average daily trading volume of 100,000 shares per day.

POWERSHARES DYNAMIC OTC PORTFOLIO

PowerShares Dynamic OTC Portfolio ETF (symbol PWO) seeks to replicate, before fees and expenses, the Dynamic OTC Intellidex Index. This index is comprised of U.S. stocks from each sector that have the greatest capital appreciation according to a proprietary Amex Intellidex Methodology. PWO offers broad general market representation with a large IT tilt. About 53 percent of the portfolio of PWO is in the IT sector.

Chapter | 11

THE IMPORTANCE OF INVESTING IN EMERGING MARKETS

As an investor or trader, you should consider gaining exposure to the faster-growing economies in the emerging markets. These markets have at times performed better than the U.S. markets. Also consider the fact that the developed non-U.S. markets have sometimes performed better than the U.S. markets.

Economically, the United States is integrated as a major player in the global economy, although many observers thought that there would be a slowdown in global trade just after September 11, 2001. It is expected that the United States will continue to expand its role as a major trading partner with the rest of the world. Nations have become more reliant on trade between nations, and this should continue. This trade has affected the currency reserves between nations. For example, non-Japanese Asian Central Banks, such as China and Korea, now hold about 40 percent of the world reserves, most of which are held in U.S. dollars.

Figure 11.1 shows the relative performance of the S&P 500 Index, the MSCI EAFE Index, and the MSCI Emerging Markets Index.

Figure 11.1

Long-Term Opportunities Exist in Emerging Markets: MSCI Emerging Markets, EAFE, S&P 500, Lehman Aggregate

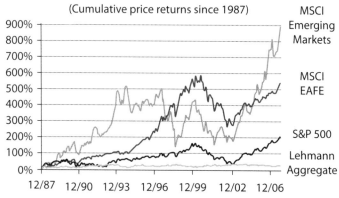

(Cumulative price returns since 1987)

MSCI Emerging Markets

MSCI EAFE

S&P 500

Lehmann Aggregate

Source: Barclays Global Investor

Emerging markets have diversity, strong economic growth, and often volatility in their capital markets. The MSCI Emerging Markets Index, shown in Figure 11.1, contains about 725 companies in approximately 25 countries. There are large and small countries in the index, with per-capita income diverse among the countries.

As you can see from Figure 11.1, an important reason to invest in emerging markets, as well as in developed foreign markets, is performance. Over a period of time, foreign markets have outperformed and portfolios with exposure to these markets have benefited.

Another reason is portfolio diversification. Although there is some correlation between developed and emerging non-U.S. stock markets and U.S. stock markets, the markets are not tied together.

The growth of trade is not limited to just one area; rather, trade is from all over the globe. China continues to grow as a global manufacturing center, spurring the growth of Asian trade. Russia has become a major energy and natural resource power, intensifying trading activities in its part of the world. The countries of Eastern Europe are developing and becoming powers.

Because there is risk to investing in developed and emerging markets around the world, you should keep your exposure to these markets in line with your risk profile.

CURRENCY RISKS OF INVESTING IN FOREIGN ETFs

Non-U.S. ETFs may have currency risks, because foreign ETFs may be traded in U.S. dollars and its investments are made in foreign equity markets. In these cases changes in the exchange rate between the U.S. dollar and the foreign currency will affect the ETF holder. Currency exposure for a U.S. investor concerns the relationship between local equity returns and the change in the value of that local currency relative to the U.S. dollar.

Read the prospectus of the foreign ETFs you invest or trade in to understand the extent of your currency risk.

THE MAJOR EMERGING MARKET: CHINA

The Chinese economy has been averaging a growth rate of 9.5 percent a year for the past 20 years (Source: Organization for Economic Co-operation and Development [OECD]; 2005 Executive Summary of the OECD assessment and recommendations; Economic Survey of China 2005). This rapid pace, among the highest in the world, is expected to continue for some time. Not only is national economic growth high, but the cultural changes it is spawning are significant. Chinese people have higher personal incomes, and the country is experiencing a concomitant reduction in poverty. China has joined the world economy to its own, and the world's, betterment.

CAPITALISM IN CHINA

Government policy has shifted to where private ownership is producing over half of China's GDP and an even higher share of exports. Private companies produce most of the new jobs and are helping the economy be more productive and profitable. The government recognizes the benefits of competition and cooperation on the world stage and continues to aid the private sector, while still developing and improving the state-owned and -operated major companies.

To further improve the banking and financing atmosphere, over two-thirds of the banking system was recapitalized recently. In addition, other reforms have improved the capacity of banks to make lending decisions based on free-market conditions. The Chinese government is continuing to develop policies to expand and deregulate further capital markets to improve the allocation of capital and lower systemic risk in the banking system.

Investors and traders miss this market at their peril. There are risks in this market, as there are in all markets, but not participating in this market due to misunderstanding it, or underestimating its potential, could be to miss an investment opportunity. Also the China market has in the past shown a low correlation to the U.S. markets, further increasing its value as an investment and hedging tool.

HALTER USX CHINA INDEX

The idea for the Halter index developed as an extension of the business the Halter Financial Group conducts in China. Halter has an office in Shanghai and has been identifying investment opportunities in that country, investing in Chinese businesses that it thought had merit, and bringing those businesses public into the U.S. capital markets.

Several years ago, in the process of compiling statistical data to quantify Chinese companies that were performing on the U.S. stock markets, Halter concluded that there were no statistics gathered of the sort needed to show that performance. Halter invested its time and capital to gather and interpret available data. From this it launched the Halter USX China Index. This index monitors the performance of companies that have the majority of their businesses in China and also have their stocks listed on U.S. stock markets.

Companies included in the Halter index are required to be listed on a U.S. exchange, either the American Stock Exchange (AMEX), Nasdaq, or the New York Stock Exchange (NYSE). The companies have the very low minimum market capitalization requirement of $50 million.

Any company that meets these requirements is listed on the index. The index, therefore, includes the entire universe of Chinese companies trading in the United States.

THE HALTER USX CHINA INDEX CONCEPT

The concept behind the index is that there are many investors and traders in the United States and around the world who are aware of China's growth and potential and want to participate but are reluctant to invest outside their own markets. This reluctance includes traders and investors in Hong Kong, who understand Chinese markets very well.

The Halter index allows investors to trade Chinese companies whose businesses are in mainland China, if the companies have agreed to fulfill the reporting obligations and listing requirements of a U.S. listing.

These listed companies are subject to the requirements of the Sarbanes-Oxley Act, as are all other listed companies. The Sarbanes-Oxley Act of 2002 was passed after a number of companies, such as Enron Corp., Tyco International, and WorldCom, Inc., collapsed, partly due to accounting scandals. This act established new or tighter standards for U.S. public company boards of directors, public accounting firms, and company managements. The financial statements of these companies are subject to U.S. standards, full SEC disclosure, and all other rigorous public filing requirements.

Glancing through the list of companies that comprise the index, one type of company stands out. These are companies that are traded in American Depositary Receipts (ADRs).

TRADING IN ADRS

An ADR is traded like a stock. It represents ownership in shares of a foreign company and is traded on U.S. markets. An ADR offers investors an opportunity to buy a foreign company without having to buy shares of that company in foreign stock markets.

Companies in the Halter USX China Index that are created in another primary market, often the Hong Kong market, are also traded on one of the U.S. exchanges. An ADR filing company, which is a foreign securities issuer, has to meet the requirements of the exchanges on which it is listing, for example, the New York Stock Exchange. The foreign company filer must also meet the exchange requirements on which it is listing, but from an SEC disclosure standpoint, the company has fewer reporting obligations than U.S. reporting companies.

About half of the Halter index companies are ADRs and half are direct exchange filers. These companies conduct half or more of their business in mainland China, are primarily listed in the United

States, and in many instances, at the holding company level, are U.S. corporations.

For example, China BAK Battery (symbol CBAK), is a Delaware corporation that owns 100 percent of a company whose entire operations are in China. From an investor perspective CBAK is the same as a U.S. company. It makes full SEC disclosure, is Sarbanes-Oxley compliant, and submits audited financial reports and all other required regulatory disclosures and reporting. Investors who buy shares are familiar with the regulations under which CBAK operates. The company operates just like a top-level U.S. company; it is fully regulatory-compliant, but its operations are in China.

Halter has found that the Chinese companies that are subject to the full disclosure requirements and are under the scrutiny of the SEC usually have a valuation premium in U.S. markets compared to companies that are listed as ADRs.

Investors and traders in the Halter index gain the opportunity to invest in China within the safety of the U.S. capital market system, whether the component companies are exchange filing companies or listed as ADRs.

Figure 11.2 shows the hypothetical performance of the Halter USX China portfolio. The ETF that attempts to replicate the performance of this index, before fees and expenses, is offered by PowerShares, and is the Golden Dragon Halter USX China (symbol PGJ).

The Halter USX China Index does not charge management fees or brokerage expenses, and no such fees or expenses were deducted from the hypothetical performance shown. The Index does not lend securities, and no revenues from securities lending were added to the performance shown. You cannot invest directly in the Index. In addition, the results actual investors might have achieved would have differed from

Figure 11.2[1]

Halter USX China Index, S&P 500, MSCI EAFE Index, and the Xinhua 25 Index, 2001 through 2007.

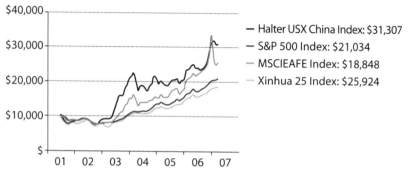

- Halter USX China Index: $31,307
- S&P 500 Index: $21,034
- MSCIEAFE Index: $18,848
- Xinhua 25 Index: $25,924

Source: PowerShares Capital Management

those shown because of differences in the timing, amounts of their investments, and fees and expenses associated with an investment in the Fund.

CAP SIZE IN THE HALTER USX CHINA INDEX

I found that about14 companies, comprising 65 percent of the index, were in the $3 to $160 billion size. These are large- and mid-cap sized companies. Approximately nine more companies were in the small-cap

---

[1] Total Returns are based on the Closing Market Price. Performance data quoted represents past performance, which is not a guarantee of future results. Investment returns and principal value will fluctuate, and shares, when redeemed, may be worth more or less than their original cost. Current performance may be higher or lower than performance data quoted. After-tax returns reflect the highest federal income tax rate but exclude state and local taxes. Fund performance reflects fee waivers, absent which, performance data quoted would have been lower.

The Halter USX China Index return does not represent the Fund return. The performance results shown are hypothetical and reflect the investment returns that might have been achieved by investing $10,000 according to the Index on May 31, 2001. The results assume that no cash was added to or assets withdrawn from the hypothetical investment and that all dividends, gains and other earnings in the account were reinvested in accordance with the Index's rules.

range, which is the $1 to $3 billion cap size. The small- to large-cap sizes comprised about 85 percent of the index. The other 15 percent was spread out over about 31 very small entrepreneurial companies, and this group is constantly changing as new companies qualify for inclusion. The Halter index is dynamic in this way.

Several of the new-generation ETFs change their constituent companies on a regular, ongoing basis. If the market price of an intelligent ETF goes up substantially, it is somewhat comforting to know that the ETF is constantly changing its companies according to its indexing methodology.

Halter did not tilt its methodology to include a number of very small, small, and medium-sized companies because they wanted to achieve this result. The result stems from the index formula, which specifies that the index picks up Chinese companies from the entire universe that meets its criteria. This trend toward a mix of very small, small, and mid-cap companies in the index will continue because Halter thinks this mix is an accurate picture of the development of the Chinese economy.

Smaller, entrepreneurial companies are important drivers of the growth of China. Many of these smaller companies were started less than 10 years ago, are reaching a mature stage, and are now qualified to go public. The state-owned companies are often slower-growth enterprises; much of the reason is attributed to their huge size. The entrepreneurial, privately owned, smaller companies are generally growing the fastest, and are thirsting for equity capital.

There are many managers in this group of small companies who are forward-looking enough to be willing to list in U.S. markets. The mindset to list in the United States is indicative of a world-class managerial outlook, revealing global aspirations.

With years of experience operating in the Chinese economy, Halter opines that the entrepreneurial U.S. listing companies will continue to be among the fastest-growing companies in China. For example, PetroChina, Ltd. (symbol PTR) is an oil and gas producer and one of the biggest Chinese companies, judged by market capitalization. It was one of the first Chinese companies to go public and has a market capitalization of about $281 billion.

The price of PetroChina has performed well, which is understandable given the increase in the price of oil. China's largest companies include oil and telecom companies, large-sized corporations.

As covered elsewhere in this book, cap-weighted indexes can perform very well, and at times outperform other ETFs. A tilt toward oil and gas, telecom, banking, and insurance companies has allowed cap-weighted Chinese indexes to achieve good returns. For example, the iShares FTSE/Xinhua China 25 Index has turned in a good performance. The index, which consists of the 25 largest, most liquid Chinese companies, has an ETF (symbol FXI).

The Halter index has an indexing methodology that fosters the inclusion of small companies. It will take many years before giant companies could dominate the index and make the weight of smaller companies in the index insignificant.

THE SAFETY OF ETF INVESTING

HOW SAFE ARE ETFS?

If you are holding an ETF that closes its shares for public trading, which some have done, you will get a liquidating distribution. This will create a tax event for you, since a liquidation is the same, for tax purposes, as if you had sold the shares. Other than the tax consequence, liquidation should cause no principal loss to you. This refers to regular 1940-Act ETFs, not some of the 1933-Act ETFs and others that might use derivatives and leverage. Check the prospectus of the ETFs to see what type of ETF you are holding or considering.

Regular ETFs do not have debts outstanding against the constituent stocks held in the portfolio and are fully equitized. When you buy an ETF, you are buying a share of a fund and you own a share in the claims of those assets. For these reasons you do not have to worry about the solvency of the issuer, since you are not buying the assets of the issuer. When an ETF is liquidated, it pays a liquidating distribution to its holders. It distributes its cash, sells off all its stocks, and pays off the holders at the NAV.

THE STATE OF THE ETF MARKET

There were about 30 ETFs worldwide when I wrote my first book about ETFs in 2000. I wrote that book because as a money manager I wanted to find a better way to invest. Empirical evidence was showing that I couldn't count on beating the market picking stocks.

I found indexing, and along with that discovered ETFs, which was the new way that indexing was being packaged—a way that was simple, brilliant, and effective. The ETF industry has moved on, to the benefit of investors and traders alike.

There are many more ETFs out there today. The AMEX recently listed a new Vanguard security class, which takes the total market to about 646 ETFs. Maybe even more impressive is that the AMEX, a major ETF exchange, had 132 new ETFs launched in 2007. There is about $620 billion invested in ETFs worldwide. Most of these assets are concentrated in the largest ETFs that are offered by major ETF makers.

There will be great growth in the ETF world in the future. Many of the current ETFs do not have large amounts of money invested in them, but they have enough to be viable. These ETFs will continue to grow as they accumulate assets.

There are only 17 ETF issuers in the market, and these issuers account for 646 worldwide ETFs. Since there are so few issuers, more issuers will probably be coming to the market, offering interesting and compelling new ETFs.

Even if there were no new issuers and the number of issuers stayed at only 17, each of these issuers could come up with five or so new ETFs a year. From that perspective it is obvious that ETF offerings will continue for the foreseeable future. However, it is likely that the pace of new offerings will slow. In 2007 there were about 169 new ETF offerings overall, more offerings than were made in 2006.

THE FUTURE OF THE ETF MARKET

It has been estimated that by 2010 there could be about $2 trillion invested in worldwide ETFs. This is not an impossibly large amount. The mutual fund market has about 10,000 mutual funds to choose from and those mutual funds have assets of about $10 trillion.

The next phase of development is the offering of actively managed ETFs, given preliminary approval by the SEC in early 2008. This may cause an increase in nonindexed ETFs. This development does not have to detract from the already created ETFs, although it will definitely increase the choices available to traders and investors, and increase the dollars deposited into the ETF market.

There are differences between actively managed ETFs and indexed ETFs. These differences should cause the quantitative indexed ETF market to continue to grow, because these ETFs give the investors and traders the advantage of seeing and understanding the disciplines backing the stock selection process. ETF buyers like this investment methodology process and the transparency of the stock selection. These features are not available with actively managed ETFs. The investors who buy actively managed ETFs are going to be buying the skill of the manager.

There may be a compromise position between these two methods of investing through the ETF system. There may be some people, for example, who believe that the RAFI, or the WisdomTree, or another approach is the most effective. Whichever approach is thought to be the most effective, many traders and investors embrace a quantitative approach. Some of the active managers will probably become accepted over time. No matter how the field shakes out, ETFs will be the investing structure of choice to deliver the best investment strategies.

INDEX

Page numbers with an f indicate figures; with an n, notes; with a t, tables.

ABOUT THE AUTHOR

Max Isaacman was a Financial Consultant at Merrill Lynch, a manager at SG Cowen, a vice president at Lehman Brothers, and performed other functions in his 40-plus years as an advisor and broker. He is a Registered Investment Advisor with East/West Securities in San Francisco, advising individuals and institutions. Isaacman was a financial columnist for the *San Francisco Examiner* and wrote for many publications, including Delta Airlines *Sky* magazine. Among his appearances are CBS *MarketWatch*, Tech TV, and the FTSE Global Index Conference, Geneva, Switzerland. Isaacman is the author of *How to be an Index Investor* (McGraw-Hill, 2000), which introduced investors to ETFs.